KAREN DOCKREY

Broadman Press
Nashville, Tennessee

4253-41
ISBN: 0-8054-5341-5

Dewey Decimal Classification: 230
Subject Headings: THEOLOGY // CHRISTIANITY
Library of Congress Catalog Card Number: 84-1702
Printed in the United States of America

Library of Congress Cataloging in Publication Data

Dockrey, Karen, 1955-
  Getting to know God.

  Includes index.
  1. Youth—Religious life.   2. Theology, Doctrinal—
Popular works—Juvenile literature.   I. Title.
BV4531.2.D6   1984   230'.044   84-1702
ISBN 0-8054-5341-5 (pbk.)

To Bill

ooooooo

my best friend
my most constant encourager
my partner in service

Using This Book

ooooooooooooooooo

You may be a person who is curious about Christianity. You may have recently become a Christian. Or perhaps you have been a Christian for several years and have some questions to which you would like answers. You may be bored and have nothing better to read. I am not sure who you are or why you have decided to read this book. Whoever you are, "Welcome!"

The one thing people who read this book have in common is that they have some questions about Christianity. I wish I could meet you personally because I know your questions are unique. I know you have special reasons for asking the questions you ask. I admire you for seeking answers. I have written this book to help you find answers to your questions.

In this book we'll explore what Christians believe, how they usually act, and how a relationship with Christ can affect your life.

Feel free to start anywhere in this book. You may want to begin by using the index to help you find information on your specific questions. You may want to choose certain chapters to read first. Of course, reading the entire book from beginning to end can lead you to a greater understanding of Christianity and of your own relationship to God.

Consider each chapter a letter to you. In these letters I have tried to explain what Christianity is and what Christians believe. I have included exercises (**Try It Out**) and questions (**Think**) to give the chapters more meaning and to help your understanding grow. I have also included Bible verses (**Check It Out**) which will help you find what God has to say. Don't just skip over these. Working the exercises, answering the questions, and reading the verses will take more time, but taking this time will help you settle the truths for yourself.

No two Christians are exactly alike. That is why you may hear many different explanations of what Christians believe. But this book is an attempt to summarize what most Christians believe most of the time. I want you to know that I understand a Christian to be a person who trusts his life to God through the person Jesus Christ. A Christian believes that Jesus is God's unique Son, God himself in human form. A Christian believes that only in God can a person find real and lasting happiness. He believes that Jesus is the most complete way that God has shown himself to people.

Why are there differences in beliefs, even among Christians? One reason is that God is difficult to put into words. He is unlimited, and words have limits. Any description of him and how he relates to his people is always less than complete. But each attempt brings us a little closer to understanding him and his ways.

Reading these chapters may cause you to think. *I hope so!* Reading these chapters may help you to find some answers. *That would be great!* It may clear up something you've never quite understood. *Good for you!* It may raise questions you never knew you had. *You won't be alone!* It may make you curious about the Bible. *Read it!* I hope that reading this book will do all of these things for you, but most of all I hope you are motivated to explore a relationship with Jesus Christ.

I challenge you to get to know God. Learn about what he has to offer you. Learn about what you have to offer him. Let yourself become involved in the most rewarding relationship available. This relationship will increase the value of every experience in your life. As the Bible says, "Whoever believes in him will never be disappointed." (1 Peter 2:6).

Contents

Contents

1

People: Why We Need God

○○○○○○○○○○○○○○○○○○○○○○○○○○○○○○○

"If only I had a boyfriend, I could be happy."
"If I had that car, I could really enjoy life."
"If my dad hadn't died, I wouldn't be so depressed all the time."
"If my brother would quit bugging me, life sure would be easier."

What would make you perfectly happy? Certain friends? A sweetheart? Unlimited money? No one bossing you around? Think for a moment about the ideal life. Write a paragraph or list five things/persons/situations that would make your life perfect.

How does thinking about you and what you want help you to get to know God? If it is true that God created you and gave you certain needs and desires, an examination of those needs and desires can tell you a lot about God.

Take a Look at Yourself

What's on your happiness list? I suspect your list may show that you:

- Need to be loved
  - Crave relationships
    - Search for happiness
      - Are not perfect
        - Have trouble doing right
          - Need power and guidance
            - Fear death

In this chapter we'll examine these needs, desires, problems, and fears. We'll discover what God does to meet them. Because he created us with these needs, he has the best ideas on what to do about them. Following his advice brings the happiness we seek.

Need Love

We all want to be loved. We all want someone to love. We will do almost anything to get people to like us. We need to know that no matter what we've done or failed to do, someone will love us. We need to know that no matter what we are like, we are loved. God knows this. He created this craving for love. He created exactly the kind of love that will fill this craving. His love is unconditional.

Check It Out: Read 1 Corinthians 13:4-7 for a description of God's kind of love.

Crave Relationships

Our need for love expresses itself in our desire for relationships. We want friends. We want sweethearts. We want a family. But just any friends, sweethearts, or family won't do. We need relationships that encourage us to be the best we can be. We need relationships in which we can both give and receive. We don't need abuse, emotional misery, and destruction. In short we need loving and healthy relationships. God knows that. That's precisely why he offers his guidance in helping us find happy relationships.

We humans need other people, and we need God. In fact, only when we establish a relationship with God can our relationships with other people be satisfying.

The best way to use a new product is to read and follow the manufacturer's instructions. Since God is our maker, following his instructions is the best way to make and keep friends, to find and maintain romance, to learn to get along with ourselves, and to succeed in any other relationship.

Consider these situations:

Jordan and Julie have been dating for some time. He is on the football team, spends all his afternoons at practice, and has to study at night. When he does have spare time, he expects Julie to be available. However, Julie is busy with her activities and is not always at home when he calls. She says that he ought to respect her schedule too.

What would God advise for this relationship? He would suggest such actions as: respect, understanding, communication, and mutual giving. Perhaps Jordan could schedule his free time far enough in advance that Julie could arrange her schedule. Perhaps Jordan and Julie could study and do other "busy" stuff together.

Elizabeth and Susan are best friends. Lately Susan has been spending lots of time with Edna, the new girl. Elizabeth feels that Susan doesn't care anymore. Susan doesn't see why she can't be friends with both girls.

What might God advise? First he would advise Elizabeth and Susan to talk. He would want them to understand each other's points of view. He would want Edna to have friends. Perhaps he would advise Elizabeth to befriend Edna too. He might help the girls to discover security in their relationship, even when other people enter the picture.

Check It Out: Some of God's guidelines for relationships are:

Friendship: Proverbs 14:29; 17:17; 18:24; 22:24-25; 27:5-6; Ecclesiastes 4:9-10; Romans 12:10,15; 15:2; 1 Corinthians 15:33.

Dating/marriage: Genesis 2:18,21-25; 1 Corinthians 11:11; Ephesians 4:29; 5:3-4, 21-33; Hebrews 10:24; 1 John 3:18.

Parent/Youth: Ephesians 6:1-4.

Search for Happiness

Every person is searching for happiness. We want the best out of life and struggle to find it. Some of the places we look are:

- money
- career
- popularity
- romance
- pleasing others
- going fun places
- success
- friends
- possessions
- clothes
- winning
- fame

Each of these brings some measure of happiness, but none is lasting or complete. None fills the empty longing for happiness and fulfillment that people have. Christians believe that within every person God has placed what might be called a "God-shaped hole." When this empty place is filled, a person feels complete. Though other things can be put into it, only God fits. Anything else leaves gaps. A man named Augustine said it like this: "The heart of man is restless until it finds rest in Thee [God]."

This emptiness expresses itself in all sorts of longings: friendship, romance, possessions, understanding, wisdom, and more. Interestingly, even if we have all of these things, they will not satisfy us unless God is there too. When God fills our empty place, he gives us these other things we need.

How does the emptiness show itself in each of these people's lives?

Anthony was adopted as an infant. Though his parents love him, he feels different and wonders if they ever want to give him back. He wonders who his natural parents are and why they gave him up for adoption. He hesitates to get close to people for fear they will reject him when they find out he is adopted.

Anthony's empty place is the need to feel unconditionally loved and accepted. He wonders why his natural parents "rejected" him and worries that others will do the same. God can fill Anthony's hole by assuring him that he (God) loves him unconditionally and that his love is perfect. He can then help Anthony accept that people will love him and assure him of his worth. He can give Anthony understanding of his adoption and confidence about the other events in his life.

Megan wants friends badly. She often lets people "use her" just so they will like her. She pays their way to ball games, gives rides all the time, lets them cheat off her paper, and even does an occasional homework assignment for someone.

Megan's empty place shows itself in her need for friends. God can fill it by being her best friend. Only he keeps all secrets, is always there, will never betray, and fully cares. When Megan accepts God, he can then give her the human friends she needs. He can teach her better friend-making and friend-keeping skills.

Cory is a high school student of average intelligence and better than average looks. He has lots of friends and seems happy all the time. He is constantly busy with school activities and gets along pretty well with his parents. He seems to have all the elements for happiness. But Cory doesn't feel that way. Something is missing, and he can't quite put his finger on it. He gets depressed when he thinks about it, so he tries to put it out of his mind.

Cory's empty place is his need for purpose. Only God can give this to him. Accepting God is more than adding another activity to his life. Rather, God will improve every area: Cory's friendships, his school work, his social life, his relationship with his parents. God can help Cory understand his feelings, can guide him in his decisions, and can make his good life even better.

Check It Out: The Bible verse Matthew 6:33 explains that when a person seeks God first, all his other needs will be given. If a person tries to fill his needs by ignoring God and simply concentrating on finding happiness in people and possessions, he will find frustration and unhappiness.

Nobody is perfect. From time to time, every person does things wrong. Sometimes wrongdoing is deliberate. Other times it is accidental. *Wrong* is anything against God. The actions/attitudes God declares wrong are those which hurt us or someone else. He makes the rules to protect us from painful consequences, not just to make rules.

Deciding just which actions are wrong is not always easy. Christians believe that God is very willing to help us discover the specific rights and wrongs in our lives.

Why bother? Why is it so important to discover and correct wrong? It's important because we can never be fully happy with wrong present in our lives. Christians call this wrong *sin*. They believe that only God can help us get rid of it.

Sins (wrongs) that people commit fall into three categories:

Deliberate sins: These are ones that we know are wrong, but we do them anyway. For example: we know it is wrong to cheat on a test, but we want the good grades so badly that we decide to cheat. These are called "sins of commission." We decide to *commit* them.

Other examples of these sins are:

- lying
- ignoring
- deceiving
- arguing
- physical violence
- robbing
- criticizing
- driving while drunk
- rejecting
- stealing
- abuse

Refusing to do right: These are good actions that we decide not to do. We know we should make friends with that new person, but we don't want other people to think we are weird. So we decide not to befriend the newcomer. These are called "sins of omission." We have *omitted doing something good.*

Some other good things we sometimes fail to do are:

- listen
- include new people
- tolerate
- be patient
- understand another's point of view
- stand up for what we believe
- give time
- cooperate
- share

Accidental sins: Sometimes we are not sure what is right or we do wrong without realizing it is wrong. A boy who wants to break up with his steady girl friend begins to avoid her. He thinks he is being nice by not telling her directly of his intentions. But his avoidance is actually more painful for her. He has wronged her without fully realizing it. We

People: Why We Need God   13

commit such sins because we are ignorant of what is right.

Some situations in which we often don't know what is right are:

- dating
- parents
- friends
- relationships

Try It Out: Think of a sin (wrong) you have done in each of these areas.

Have Trouble Doing Right

"How can we avoid doing wrong if there are so many ways to do it?" The Bible says that as human beings we can't avoid wrong altogether. However, there are ways to greatly reduce our sinning.

Not being able to avoid wrong completely is known as "our sinful nature." Given a chance, every person will choose to do wrong sometimes. We humans make the excuse that it is all right to do wrong in certain circumstances. We fail to accept the fact that wrong is wrong and wrong hurts. We think it may be wrong for others, but we can get away with it. Sometimes, we are simply rebellious. We don't want God to tell us what to do. We want to try wrong to see what it is like.

One of the problems with wrongdoing (sin) is that one sin leads to another. Once we begin, it is hard to stop. Cheating seemed an easy way for Brad to make a high grade when he was too busy to study for the test. Once he failed to study for the one test, he was behind in studying for the next one. Cheating had worked before, so he tried again. This time he got caught. When he was accused of cheating, he lied to keep from being punished. Gradually he lost his motivation to study. Because he had not learned the material during the first part of the course, he was so far behind that now he could make good grades only if he cheated. He began to lose confidence in his ability. He stopped trying to succeed through learning the material. He had learned to give into pressures that hadn't even tempted him before. Cheating led to lying which led to loss of motivation, loss of confidence, and continued cheating.

Even when we realize that we are doing wrong, it is often hard to stop. Evil seems to have an almost physical hold on us. We want to stop, but instead we continue to hurt ourselves and others.

So what is the solution? The only one who can help us break this frustrating pattern of doing wrong is God. Only his power and love are strong enough. Through his Son, Jesus Christ, who gave his life and through the power of his Holy Spirit, God destroys sin's hold on us.

We Need Power and Guidance

The first step to breaking sin's hold is to become a Christian. This starts God's power flowing through a person. God gives each new Christian a fresh start. He receives a totally new nature which is eager and able to do good. This nature is capable of happiness because it comes from God.

Once you are a Christian, God's power can help you reduce your pattern of doing wrong. Some ways are:

1. Try doing right, and notice the positive results.

2. Take the time to learn what is right to avoid "accidental sins." This information can be found in the Bible.

3. Find friends who do right and hang around them. They will influence you in a positive way.

God's plan for fighting sin includes giving you a good action to put in place of the sinful one. He works with Christians constantly to guide them into right action, and thus happy, living.

Even as a Christian you will fight with sin. Your old nature continues to enjoy sinning. You continue to be tempted. God's Holy Spirit, who lives in each Christian, gives the power to fight this desire to sin. It is a lifelong battle, but it can be won. For ideas on how to fight temptation, see the temptation section in the chapter "The Christian Life: Growing."

Check It Out: 2 Corinthians 5:17 speaks of a Christian becoming a new person.

Romans 7:14 to 8:2 describes the frustration which results from trying to break sin habit on our own.

You Will Die

Few people enjoy talking about death. Why? We don't want to die. We don't want to experience its pain. We don't want to leave the people we love. We don't know what awaits us after death. We fear death.

Christians believe that God provides an answer to this scary dilemma. They believe God has prepared a new kind of life for his people after death. After they die on earth, God will raise them from death in a new form. They will be reunited with their loved ones and will live with God forever in a place called heaven. In this place there is no sadness, pain, or suffering. This life after death is called *eternal life*, and it is some Christians' favorite benefit of Christianity.

Most Christians still aren't excited about dying. However, knowing that God will raise them from death makes facing it easier. They still miss their loved ones who die. They still cry at funerals. But they understand that death and funerals have a measure of hope. They know that life is not over but simply that life has now entered a new dimension. They know they will be reunited.

Check It Out: John 14:1-4 tells about the place that Jesus is preparing for Christians.

First Corinthians 15:20,35-44,51-58 explain what being raised from death will be like.

First Thessalonians 4:13-18 speaks of the hope that mourning Christians have.

God Can Meet Our Needs

Every person has needs and desires. These have been explored in this chapter. God can meet them for us by:
- Loving us unconditionally
  - Relating to us individually and personally
    - Guiding us toward happy relationships with people
      - Filling us with more happiness and contentment than we ever dreamed possible
        - Breaking sin's hold on us through Jesus Christ
          - Teaching us right from wrong through the Bible, through a relationship with him, and through other Christians
            - Giving us power to do right and avoid wrong
              - Assuring us of life with him after death

God and Me?

Think about yourself specifically once again for a moment.
Name three things you like to do.
Name three things you *don't* like to do.
List five of your positive qualities.
List five of your negative qualities.

Name five words which describe your roles/relationships (examples: brother, student, daughter).

Describe your physical appearance.

The things you like to do, don't like to do, your qualities, your relationships, and your appearance combine to make up the person you are. Being a Christian is more than adding another quality, a new physical characteristic, or something more to do. Becoming a Christian is allowing Jesus Christ to enter your life and influence every part of you. Jesus can make the things you like even more fun. He can make the things you don't like to do more bearable. He can help you add to your positive qualities and subtract from your negative ones. He can help your relationships run more smoothly. He can even improve your physical appearance by helping you to be a happier person which will show in your face.

As you read this book, think about how God could affect you: your life, your relationships, and your activities.

Think: In what area of your life do you feel the need for God most strongly? If you are a Christian: In what area has God made the greatest difference? Where do you think he should work next?

2
God: What He Is Like

○○○○○○○○○○○○○○○○○○○○○○○○○

"Why am I here?" "What gives my life meaning?"
"What started the universe?"
"What keeps the world going? Why does it work the way it does?"
"Where will it all end?"
"Is there someone or something worth committing my life to?"
These are some of the many questions people ask about life.
Different people have answered these questions in different ways.
Christians feel that God is the right answer to each of them. Let's look
at some of the facts which lead them to this conclusion.

There are five good places to learn about God: creation (the way the
world is), human nature, the Bible, the person Jesus Christ, and one's
personal experience.

The World Tells Us About God

Look out your window. What do you see? Trees? Sunshine? Rain?
People talking? Think of the people, the animals, the plants, the
weather, all the aspects of the earth. How did they get here? Just
happen one day? Evolve from a single cell? If so, where did that cell
come from? How did the cell know to multiply and to change? What
determined the patterns in which the cells arranged themselves? Why
are there giraffes and humans rather than creatures with no noses?
How can we explain the uniqueness of each person?

It has been estimated that the scientific probability for all the
fascinating things in this world to have happened completely by chance
is one in ten to the 40,000th power. That's a one with 40,000 zeroes
behind it. Therefore, it is highly unlikely that the detail, personality,

and order of this earth came from an accidental or impersonal process. The nature of this world requires a creator. Christians believe God is this Creator and that he gives each part of the world its purpose.

A famous illustration is told about a man who found a pocket watch in a field. He had never seen a watch before, and it amazed him. It made a rhythmic sound, and the hands moved in harmony with the sun. Where did such an instrument come from? He concluded that someone had to have made it. It was too intricate, precise, and unusual to have simply happened. He understood that a watch requires a watchmaker.

Likewise, the world with all its detail requires a creator. This Creator is God. Romans 1:20 states that we can know God through nature: "Ever since God created the world, his invisible qualities, both his eternal power and his divine nature, have been clearly seen; they are perceived in the things that God has made."

Think: How would you explain characteristics of the world we live in if they did not come from God?

Human Nature Teaches About God

Think about the people you know. How are they designed? How are they alike? How are they different? What can they do?

People have personality. They think, act, feel, and decide. They are not automated robots. Each has his own special way of talking, worrying, having fun, doing interesting things, and relating to others. Christians believe that such personality could have only originated from a personal source. An impersonal rock could not have generated the intricate and individual beings that humans are. A person can create something impersonal like a painting or a bologna sandwich, but something impersonal cannot create personality.

The personal nature of people indicates that there must be a personality who created them. Christians believe that this creative personality is God.

The human sense of right and wrong is also a strong evidence for God's existence.

Name three things that are wrong and three things that are right.

You probably had no difficulty doing this. Each of us has a sense of what is right and what is wrong. We live by this standard and expect others to treat us according to it. For example, we know that it is right to be concerned about people and that it is wrong to cheat on our friends. We know it is wrong to steal or kill. We feel that giving deserves giving in return.

People who cheat on their friends don't argue that cheating is right. Instead, they state why they have an excuse for disobeying the standard this once. "I cheated on him because he cheated on me!" People who steal say, "They dared me!" A murderer might say, "She was going to betray me!" People know their behavior is wrong. They simply decide not to do what they know they should.

Granted, there are differences over some areas of right and wrong. Examples are: whether to cheat on a test, whether to obey parents in certain situations, and whether to build nuclear weapons. But each group does have a standard. Even the most crazed psychopath wants to be treated fairly.

Where does this standard of moral behavior come from? Because of its consistency (There is worldwide agreement on certain principles.) and universality (Everyone has a code of right and wrong.), it must come from a single source. How can you explain this sense of oughtness without a source? Christians believe the only possible explanation is that God created it.

Think: Do you have any other explanation?

The Bible Describes God

The Bible is an even more reliable source of information about God than creation and human nature because it is less open to individual opinion. It is straightforward and clear. As the chapter on the Bible states, there is a great deal of evidence for its authority. The Bible is the Book which tells about God and the ways he responds to people. It illustrates the actions, emotions, and words of God.

The Bible speaks of God in personal terms. He is not simply a "great force" or the "power behind the world" but rather One who thinks, acts, and feels. He is very interested in the actions and attitudes of his people. Some of the words the Bible uses to describe God are:

Love: (1 John 4:8-12,16)   Word: (John 1:1-4)
Spirit: (John 4:24)   Light: (1 John 1:5)
Power: (Ephesians 6:10)   Shelter: (Psalm 62:5-8)

Comfort: (Isaiah 66:13)	Guidance: (Proverbs 3:5-6)
Eyes: (Proverbs 15:3)	Protector: (Psalm 121:3-8)
Peace: (Isaiah 26:3; Romans 8:6)	Freedom: (Romans 8:2)
Rest: (Matthew 11:28-30)	Forgiveness (1 John 1:9)

The most powerful and most familiar of these word pictures is *love*. There are many definitions of love. But only God describes real love. His kind of love is based on actions rather than feelings. According to 1 Corinthians 13, God's kind of love includes:

patience	no jealousy
kindness	no boasting
protection	no pride
trust	no rudeness
hope	no selfishness
happy with the truth	no quick anger
constant faithfulness	no record of wrongs
eternalness	no happiness with evil

Jesus Models What God Is Like

A group of ants diligently builds its home in the field. You watch them with fascination on your lunch break. As part-time help on the farm you realize that the field will be plowed the next day. Having come to admire the ants, you try to direct them to build elsewhere. You scoop them up and move them. They go back. You try to transfer the anthill. They rebuild in the original site. You talk to them, but they don't cooperate. You feel helpless to warn them of the impending danger. You think, "If only I were an ant, they would understand me."

God has solved a similar communication problem with us by becoming a human. This human is Jesus Christ. Jesus is a form of God we can understand. The best way to know about someone is for that person to tell you about himself. God has done just that through the person Jesus.

The Bible says, "Christ is the visible likeness of the invisible God" (Colossians 1:15). "For it was by God's own decision that the Son has in himself the full nature of God" (Colossians 1:19).

By observing the way Jesus treated people, handled problems, and faced difficulties, we can learn what God is like. Jesus lived the type of life God wants each person to live. While Jesus lived on earth, he had every human characteristic, including human limitations. Because he was like us, he understands just what we go through (Hebrews 2:17-18). The chapter "Jesus: God in Human Form" gives more detail about Jesus.

Personal Experience Puts Us in Touch with God

Uncountable numbers of people have said, "I know without a doubt that God exists because he is real in my life. My relationship with him is unmistakable proof of his existence."

Many, many people have been transformed by God. Their lives are dramatically different after encountering him. Cruel people become kind. Cowards develop great personal strength and become willing to risk their lives for their convictions. The personal experiences of these people are strong evidence that God is real.

Personal experience is a powerful measure of truth. We know the stove is hot when we have been burned by it. Likewise, we can know that God exists and is forgiving, patient, and personal when we experience those qualities in a relationship with him.

Personal experience, however, is not foolproof. When we come in from the cold, cold water feels warm on our hands. In this instance, our experience has given us an inaccurate picture of the way things are. Similarly, a person who has had an unhappy relationship with an earthly father, may want nothing to do with God who is sometimes called heavenly Father. Our experiences with God must constantly be checked against what the Bible says about him.

Youth Define God's Characteristics

Some Christian youth have described God this way:

"He is strength and comforting. He fills the empty spots. I don't feel alone with God."

"He is a helpful person who loves us for what we are. He is caring and loving."

"He is our Creator, our Father, our Helper."

"He is love. He is the Forgiver of sins."

"He is powerful and strongly desires us to follow his ways."

"He's the Spirit who created me and takes care of me. His care includes happiness, love, peace, and eternal life."

"He's understanding."

"He's flawless, perfect."

These word pictures help humans understand and describe the indescribable God. Many people try to describe God's physical characteristics. They see him as a cloud, a spirit, or a grandfatherly figure with a long white beard. But Jesus has said that God is spirit (John 4:24). Though we would like to describe him, God has no physical form as we know it.

How Can We Know God Exists?

There is an enormous amount of evidence which says that God is real. Some of this evidence has been discussed in this chapter. Interestingly, people who say there is no God have not been able to prove it. The evidence for God's existence is much stronger than that against it.

Think: Christians believe there is a God. What do you think? What are your reasons for believing that he exists?

So What Is He Like?

Based on creation, human nature, the Bible, Jesus Christ, and personal experience, Christians believe that God is
Personal
All-loving
All-good
All-powerful
All-knowing.
They believe that he
wants the best for people
allows people to choose or reject him
allows people to act rightly or wrongly
has created the best possible world
does all he can to make people happy
desires a relationship with each person.

God and Me

Think: Think for a moment about God. What is your idea of him? What do you think is his idea of you?

Did you know that he thinks about you quite often and would like to get to know you better? He is interested in the details of your life. He

God: What He Is Like **23**

wants to help you have a life that is satisfying. In fact, he knows better than anyone else just how you can be happy.

So What?

What if God exists? What if he really has the qualities that Christians believe he does? What difference does that make to you?

Since God exists and really does care for you, you have a great deal to gain by getting to know him. He offers you a relationship with him with such benefits as

- Contact with the source of happiness
- Power to handle problems
- Guidelines for forming and keeping happy relationships
- Guidance in making decisions
- A sense of peace that makes your good circumstances better and your bad circumstances less painful.

Try It Out: For one month, give God a chance. Try to communicate with him in these two ways:

1. *Pray.* Your prayer does not have to be fancy or even confident. You might pray: "Well God, I'm not even sure if you are there but if you are, I want to try to get to know you. Show me a bit of yourself and help me to understand who you are. Thanks."

2. *Read the Bible.* The Bible is God's personal letter to you. Read the Book of John, one chapter at a time. Open your mind to what God is saying to you.

P.S.: Caution! A great deal of harm can result from an inaccurate image of God. Be sure that the God you choose to believe in, or not to believe in, is the One who exists. For example, many people refuse to believe in a God who causes wars and sends people to hell. The God I know hates war and hell. People, not God, cause war. People, not God, choose to go to hell.

Second, some people have a very unhappy homelife. When they hear God called heavenly father, they think of their own cruel or uncaring parent. They want nothing to do with this God. Comparing God to humans can be helpful, but be certain that you chose humans who reflect God's qualities. Remember: we were made like God, not he like us.

A final example: many people feel that God cannot forgive them for a wrong they have committed. They live their lives in lonely fear of God's anger. The person who feels that God does not forgive him may actually be having trouble forgiving himself. God has already forgiven. The only unforgivable sin is refusing to accept God and his love (Matthew 12:32; Luke 12:10).

3

Jesus: God in Human Form

○○○○○○○○○○○○○○○○○○○○○○○○○○○○○○○○○

Here are some words which have been used to describe Jesus.
Choose the ones you think are accurate.

Teacher	Fanatic	Fake
Religious Leader	Good Man	Great Teacher
God	Carpenter	Lord
Son of God	The Way	The Truth

History confirms that the man Jesus lived. We know that he was born, lived, and died in the Middle East. We know that his birthplace was Bethlehem, his hometown was Nazareth, and much of his teaching took place in the city of Jerusalem. He was Jewish. He had an earthly father, mother, brothers, and sisters. His earthly father, Joseph, was a carpenter, a profession Jesus learned. Jesus lived for thirty-three years and died by crucifixion.

What Do Christians Understand About Jesus?

Christian youth use the following words for Jesus:

- Loving
- Comforting
- The Only Way
- Caring
- Nonjudgmental
- Considerate
- Nice
- Kind
- Perfect

They describe him like this:

"A helpful person who was willing to die for us."

"Someone who died for our sins so we could live."

"He's warm, loving, like a friend or a brother."

"The Son of God."

"An innocent outsider trying to help us see the light."

"A perfect man, dedicated to God and concerned about people."

Jesus' Life and Ministry

The Bible tells us about Jesus from many perspectives. It describes Jesus through his own words about himself, through his actions, and through others' words about him. The most accurate picture of Jesus may be gained through reading the first four books of the New Testament (Matthew, Mark, Luke, and John). These books are called the Gospels, which means the good news about Jesus.

Jesus was born to a young Jewish woman named Mary. Jesus' father is God himself. Christians refer to this as the virgin birth. Jesus was conceived by a miraculous process that only God completely understands. Jesus is the only person to have ever been conceived this way.

Mary was engaged to marry a man named Joseph. At first, Joseph did not believe that Mary's pregnancy was from God. He thought she had been with another man. But in a very special dream, God assured him of the truth. So Joseph and Mary were married. Joseph became Jesus' earthly father.

Jesus was born in the city of Bethlehem in Judea (in the Middle East). He was born while his parents were on a trip to their hometown. Because there were no vacant rooms in the local inn, Jesus was born in a stable and laid in a manger (feed trough). Many people visited the baby Jesus, convinced that he was God's Son. Some of these were shepherds and Wise Men. Some of the religious people were delighted to see him. They had been awaiting his birth for a long time. Not everyone, however, believed that this baby was God. Many religious leaders doubted him. King Herod tried to have him killed because he feared that Jesus would become king and take over his kingdom.

The Bible does not give us many details about Jesus' early childhood. We know that he had many of the same experiences of any young person and that he grew both physically and mentally. We assume that he helped his father in the carpenter shop.

Jesus' earthly ministry began when he was about thirty. His first step was to be baptized. After his baptism, the Holy Spirit came down to him from heaven. God's voice said, "You are my own dear Son. I am pleased with you." (Luke 3:22). Shortly after Jesus' baptism, he

Jesus: God in Human Form 27

was tempted by the devil. He resisted these and all other temptations in his life.

During his ministry, Jesus loved, taught, healed, and forgave people. He accepted and associated with people who were considered unacceptable. He taught about God by using illustrations, stories, parables, and Scriptures. He also taught by the way he lived and the way he treated people. He healed physical, emotional, and spiritual diseases. He forgave people their sins (wrongs), a privilege reserved for God.

Jesus got himself in trouble with some of the religious leaders because he mixed with social outcasts and nonreligious people. He went to their parties and houses. Sometimes these people were more open to learning from Jesus than the religious people. The religious and socially acceptable people thought they didn't need Jesus.

Eventually, the religious leaders became so frustrated with Jesus that they had him killed by crucifixion by the political authorities. They felt that he was wrongly interpreting God and that he was threatening their own religious power. Little did they know that Jesus understood the way religion really should be.

After Jesus had been dead three days, God raised him from death. This is called the resurrection. He appeared to various groups of his followers. He stayed on earth and communicated with his followers for forty days. Then he was taken into heaven and continues to live there with God.

Soon after Jesus was taken to heaven, the Holy Spirit was sent to believers. Through his Spirit, God continues to communicate with Christians as he did through Jesus (see the chapter "Holy Spirit: Guide for Living").

His Impact

The earthly ministry of Jesus lasted only three years. In those three years he changed the course of history. Countless people have become his followers. These followers are called Christians. Today Jesus continues to transform people and the way they live. The far-reaching influence of this man indicates that there was something very special about him. Christians believe this special quality is that he is God.

Check It Out: Read about the birth, life, and death of Jesus in the Bible books Matthew, Mark, Luke, and/or John.

Titles of Jesus

The Bible gives many titles for Jesus. These help us understand his character and purpose:

Lord: Lord means "master." The Christian belongs to Jesus. Because he is God, Jesus has the authority to make decisions in the Christian's life (Matthew 7:21-27; 11:29-30).

The Christ: Christ means the "Messiah" or the One sent by God. Jesus was and is God's unique messenger (John 16:16).

Forgiver of sins: this privilege was reserved for God. Because Jesus was God, he could forgive sins (Luke 5:20-21).

The way to God: Jesus claimed to be "the way, the truth, and the life." The answers to life's questions are found in him (John 14:1-14).

Teacher: Jesus' words and advice are trusted by the Christian. They listen to him and do what he says (John 3:2).

Door/gate: Jesus is the door to God (John 10:7-10).

The good shepherd: Jesus gave his life for us, his sheep. Like a shepherd, he takes care of his people and meets all their needs (John 10:14-15; Psalm 23).

The resurrection: Jesus is our hope for life after death. Because he was raised from death, Christians will also be raised from death (John 11:25).

The Uniqueness of Jesus: Both God and Human

Jesus is the only major religious leader who has claimed to be God. Neither Buddha, Brahma, Muhammad, nor any other great religious leader has made this claim. Current religious leaders may claim to be Jesus Christ or a second Jesus, but none claim to be God himself.

Other religious leaders teach that they know the truth about the universe or the way to God. But Jesus stated that *he* is the truth and *he* is the way to God.

Jesus was just like any other human. He was fully human, yet he also had all the characteristics of God. As a human, he was born, lived, and died. He had parents, brothers, and sisters. He was tempted. He ate, slept, worked, and related to people. He felt hungry, tired, happy, sad, pain, heat, cold, lonely, loved.

As the Son of God, he lived exactly as God would live as a person. He never gave into temptation and never sinned. He had God's wisdom. He expressed this through his teaching and his work with people. He had God's power. He showed it through forgiving sins, curing illnesses, changing the weather, and overpowering evil. He lived God's kind of love by meeting needs and by understanding people of all social classes, sexes, and religious backgrounds. He expressed God's love by dying for all humans.

Check It Out: As a human, Jesus fully understands what we go through. Read Hebrews 2:17-18 and 4:15-16.

Philippians 2:5-11 speaks about Jesus being God and man.

He Is Lord

Christians believe that the most important characteristic about Jesus is that he actually is God. Almost any person, Christian or non-Christian, would admit that Jesus was a good man and a moral teacher. But a Christian writer named C. S. Lewis has explained why Jesus cannot be simply a good moral teacher. He has to be Lord (God) or he was a liar or was mentally ill. Being simply a good moral teacher is not an option. A good moral teacher would not have claimed to be God if he was not.

Jesus claimed to be God. He stated that he was God's Son and that he and the Father were one. He explained that he was the great "I Am" which was the name for God in Hebrew. He claimed that others were sinners but not he himself. Only God would be completely sinless.

Jesus claimed to be God and acted like God. If he were not God, then he had to be crazy or lying.

What do we think of people who claim to be God today? We lock them up in mental hospitals and label them as mentally ill. Maybe Jesus was mentally ill. If so, he would have had other characteristics that accompany mental illness. But he was not disoriented. He was clearly in touch with reality. He had healthy relationships. He functioned well even under great stress. Jesus' life-style clearly indicates that he was not mentally ill.

Perhaps Jesus was lying. Perhaps Jesus claimed to be God even though he knew he was not God. But if he were lying, his lie got him into big trouble. He was rejected, tortured, and crucified. If he had been lying, he surely would not have suffered and died for it. Once the heat was on, he would have admitted his joke. But he didn't. Jesus suffered and died.

The third option remains. If Jesus were not mentally ill and if he were not lying, he had to be Lord. He was and is actually who he claimed to be—God himself. His authority, wisdom, miracles, and power indicate that this is the only option. One can decide to accept or to reject Jesus, but one cannot decide who he was. The evidence strongly indicates that he was and is God.

Check It Out: Some of Jesus' claims to be God are recorded in John 11:25-27; Mark 14:61-62; and Luke 4:16-21.

The Resurrection

Christians believe that after Jesus died God raised him to life again and that he has been alive ever since. This is called the resurrection.

The resurrection is central to the faith of Christians because it assures them that they too will be raised from death.

Many people have tried to prove that the resurrection didn't really happen. In the process of investigation, many who set out to disprove the resurrection have ended up convinced that it really did happen. The evidence is strong.

The empty tomb is one of the convincing proofs. Only the resurrection can explain the empty tomb. Some propose that the tomb was empty because the disciples stole the body. Others claim that the Roman or Jewish authorities stole the body. Still others claim that Jesus didn't die but revived from a faint and left the tomb. None of these possibilities can be supported.

The disciples would have stolen the body for one reason: to make it look like Jesus had really been raised, even though he hadn't. But the disciples did not understand when Jesus told them he was going to rise from death. They did not see its importance. Even if they had stolen the body, the disciples underwent great hardship to the point of death as a result of their belief in Jesus. They would not have done that for a lie.

Jesus: God in Human Form 31

The Roman or Jewish authorities would have stolen the body to prove that Jesus really did *not* rise from the dead. If they had stolen the body, they would have produced it as evidence to silence those who claimed his resurrection.

Jesus himself could not have walked from the tomb and faked his resurrection. A huge boulder covered the entrance to the tomb. He would not have been able to move it by himself, especially in his weakened condition. Several armed guards also were stationed at the tomb. He could not have fought them off. Even if he had, the guards would have told the story.

Others try to disprove the resurrection by stating that the biblical writers made up the whole story. But the biblical account has too many peculiarities to be a fake. If the story had been made up, it would not have included women discovering Jesus' resurrection. (At that time, the testimony of women was not respected.) Second, it would have made the disciples look like heroes instead of cowards. (They ran when Jesus was arrested and crucified.) Third, it would have made Jesus out to be a political hero, the type leader they hoped for, rather than a quiet winner—the leader he was. A "made-up" Bible would be of a completely different nature than the one we have.

Other evidences for the truth of the resurrection are the many eyewitnesses who saw Jesus alive after he had been killed.

Check It Out: Read about the resurrection in Matthew 28; Mark 16; Luke 24; and John 20—21. First Corinthians 15:3-8 tells about the people he appeared to. First Corinthians 15:12-19,35-44,55-56 helps to explain its significance.

The Second Coming

Jesus told his disciples that one day he would come back to earth to take all the Christians to heaven. When he returns, the world as we know it will end and a new heaven and a new earth will be established. This gives Christians great hope. It helps them get through hard times and helps them know that evil will end.

There is a great deal of mystery and intrigue surrounding this subject. Many Christians spend much time and energy investigating when Christ will come back, what it will be like, and how the world will end. Just as we do not understand the precise details about how the world began, we do not understand exactly how it will end. Christians keep trying to understand the details. In the meantime, they find assurance in knowing that no matter what happens, Christ will take care of them.

Many Christian groups have tried to predict the day the world will end. Some have even moved into the mountains or sold their possessions in preparation for Christ's return on a certain day. But Jesus said not even he himself knew the day (Mark 13:32).

Check It Out: The following verses teach about Christ's second coming: Acts 1:9-11 (he will come back); John 14:3 (he has gone to prepare a place); and Revelation 21:1-4 (There will be a new heaven and new earth.)

Why Did Jesus Christ Come?

Christians believe that Jesus has been alive since the beginning of time. They believe that at a time especially chosen by God, he was born as a human baby on earth to show people what God is like and what they should be like. God is beyond human comprehension, but Jesus is understandable. The people who lived when Jesus lived observed the way he treated people, handled problems, resisted evil, and enjoyed life. They were inspired by God to write this down. These writings became the Bible in which we can read about Jesus today. By imitating him, we can live God's kind of life.

Jesus also came to bring humans and God back together again. For many years people had been ignoring God and refusing to live in relationship with him. Jesus' life and death were a testimony of God's love for humans. He helped people understand that only in relationship with God could they be satisfied with life.

Jesus taught people about himself and about God. He did this through talking, through the way he treated people, and through the way he responded to situations. He explained that only through himself could people be united to God. He called himself the "door," the "way," the "truth," and the "light."

Jesus came to die for us. He received the treatment that we deserve. Even though many people misunderstood Jesus, mistreated him, and even killed him, he continued to love.

The unconditional love that people crave is found in Jesus. His kind of love produces change in people. By accepting Jesus as God and by committing themselves to live in relationship with him, people become Christians.

Check It Out: John 1:1-5 explains that Jesus has been alive since the beginning of time. John 1:14 describes his becoming a human. In these passages Jesus is called "the Word."

Philippians 2:6-11 describes the changes Jesus went through to become human.

Romans 8:1-4 explains why Jesus came.

Think: What have you discovered new about Jesus? What about him still confuses you? Ask a Christian you know to explain it.

Summary

Christians identify with Jesus and try to pattern their lives after him. They believe:

He is God in human form;

He is the Lord and Guide of life;

He understands how it is to live as a human;

He died and was raised from death;

He is the way to God;

He will come back.

4
The Holy Spirit: God in Us

You have read about God and about his Son, Jesus Christ (God in human form). It may seem a bit confusing that both of these are God. But hang on. We are not through yet! Christians also believe in God, the Holy Spirit. The Holy Spirit is God who lives within each Christian.

Why do Christians have three gods? They are not actually three gods, but three forms of God. Christians believe that the idea came from God himself. The concept is called the Trinity or the Triune God which means "God in three persons/forms." Christians believe that in order for us to experience God fully, we experience him in three forms. Each is fully God, but each is different in purpose.

The following illustrations can help your understanding of God in three forms. Choose the one that makes the most sense to you:

● God is like water. Water comes in solid (ice), liquid (water), and gas (steam). Each is H_2O (the chemical name for water), but each is different. Each has special functions. Ice is cooling, water refreshes thirst, and steam helps cleanse our bodies and clear our lungs.

● God is like a man. He is a father to his child, a husband to his wife, and a brother to his sister. The man is the same in each relationship, but he relates to each person differently.

If you still feel a bit confused about the three natures of God (the Trinity), do not be overly concerned. It is a complicated concept that even mature Christians have difficulty understanding. Simply try to grasp that God works in three forms, and each is God.

Who Is the Holy Spirit?

The Holy Spirit is the form of God which lives within each Christian. The Holy Spirit guides, comforts, counsels, and convicts.

How can the Holy Spirit be in each person? He is not limited by time and space as we humans are. He can be more than one place at a time. He can talk to more than one person at once. He can guide every Christian at the same time.

Jesus said in John 14—16 that the Holy Spirit would:
- come from the Father (God)
- be a "Helper"
- stay with each Christian forever
- reveal the truth about God
- be within Christians
- speak about Jesus
- guide people to understand sin, right, and judgment
- lead Christians into all truth
- take what Jesus said and tell it to Christians

Check It Out: A concise description of the Holy Spirit can be found in John 14:16-17; 15:26; 16:7-8,13-15.

First Corinthians 3:16 explains that the Holy Spirit lives within Christians.

What Is He Like?

The Holy Spirit does not have human form as does Jesus. At the same time, he is not some ghostly, cloudy gas. He is a person with a nonphysical form. He has personality. He thinks, acts, feels, and relates. He has all the qualities of God. He constantly works to show people why God's ways are best and how to live them. He gives Christians power to live God's life-style.

What Does the Holy Spirit Do?

The Holy Spirit is the Christian's helper. He is a day-by-day, situation-by-situation guide. He helps in four ways: you can more easily remember these functions of the Holy Spirit by noticing that they all begin with C.

The Holy Spirit performs these functions in several ways. He speaks through the Bible, through a strong feeling of right/wrong, and through other Christians. He is like a "divine conscience." As the Christian grows he learns how to distinguish between his own thoughts and those of the Holy Spirit.

He *Convicts*: the Holy Spirit helps Christians understand when they are doing right and when they are doing wrong. When they are doing right, he encourages them to continue. When they are doing or about to do wrong, he points out the wrong action/attitude, how it will hurt the Christian or someone else, and how to change it.

He *Comforts*: When Christians encounter sadness, frustrations, or hard situations, the Holy Spirit comforts. He helps Christians feel loved when they feel no one cares. He understands when they have done poorly on a test or when a friend lets them down. He comforts them when they realize they have done something wrong and feel badly. However, the Holy Spirit does not stop with simple comfort. He gives God's strategy for improving the situation.

He *Communicates*: The Holy Spirit is the Christian's "hot line" to God. He explains God's truths to the Christian and helps the Christian to put those truths into practice. He does this by helping him to find information from the Bible or from other Christians. Because the Holy Spirit knows fully both the mind of God and the mind of humans, he is able to counsel and communicate very effectively.

He is the *Courage-Giver*: The Holy Spirit empowers Christians. He gives them the power to live God's way, to stand up for what is right, to resist temptation, to speak for God, and to enjoy living in every kind of circumstance. His power is not spectacular and showy. Instead, it is steady and strong. It always points the Christian to God.

Check It Out: First Corinthians 2:9-11 explains why the Holy Spirit is qualified to convict, comfort, communicate, and give courage.

How Does He Come?

The Holy Spirit came to Jesus' followers on the day of Pentecost following Jesus Christ's death and resurrection. Pentecost was a Jewish holy period that was celebrated each year. During Pentecost, Jewish believers expressed their thanks to God for a bountiful harvest.

The coming of the Holy Spirit was a spectacular occasion. A group of believers were together when suddenly there was a loud noise which sounded like a strong wind. It filled the whole house. They saw what looked like tongues of fire. These spread out and seemed to touch each person in the room.

The believers began to talk in foreign languages through the power of

The Holy Spirit: God in Us 37

the Holy Spirit. Needless to say, onlookers were both amazed and confused. They were people of all nationalities, and each heard the believers talking in his own language.

Some of the observers thought that the believers were drunk and just acting crazy! A believer named Peter stood up and explained that they were not drunk but that the Holy Spirit had come and given this expression of communication. Peter reminded them about Jesus and gave details about who Jesus really was. Many became believers after hearing Peter's talk.

Check It Out: Read Acts 2:1-42 for the details about the Holy Spirit's coming to Jesus' disciples.

Today the Holy Spirit's coming is not as spectacular but it is just as powerful. He comes to live in every Christian the minute he or she becomes a Christian. He begins to teach the new Christian about God and to empower him to live God's way. This power expresses itself in the ability to recognize and overcome wrong, to live a happy life, and to have good relationships with God and other people. The Holy Spirit brings God's kind of happiness. This happiness remains no matter what the outward circumstances.

The Holy Spirit is the seal of the new Christian's relationship with God. As the Bible explains: "You believed in Christ, and God put his stamp of ownership on you by giving you the Holy Spirit he had promised. The Spirit is the guarantee that we shall receive what God has promised his people, and this assures us that God will give complete freedom to those who are his" (Ephesians 1:13-14).

Check It Out: Acts 2:38 and 10:44-47 are two instances when the Holy Spirit came to new believers.

Evidence of His Presence

The Holy Spirit's presence in the believer causes positive changes. These changes are called the "fruit of the Holy Spirit." You recognize an apple tree because it bears apples. Likewise, you recognize the presence of the Holy Spirit in a Christian by the "fruit of the Holy Spirit." This fruit, as listed in Galatians 5:22-23 are:

love	patience	faithfulness
joy	kindness	humility

peace	goodness	self-control

Some of the "fruit" of life without God are:

frustration	jealousy	lack of love for others
guilt	worry	critical spirit
loneliness	impatience	selfishness

The Bible encourages Christians to let the Holy Spirit express the fruit of the Spirit through them. The Holy Spirit is not a "bully." He shows his power only when allowed to do so. This is one reason some Christians appear to have more of these qualities than others. They have learned to let the Holy Spirit control them.

Think: Which list of characteristics (fruit) would you rather have in your life? Why?

Gifts of the Spirit

The Holy Spirit also gives gifts. Though each Christian has the opportunity to bear the same "fruit," not all have the same gifts. Each Christian has gifts. A Christian uses his gift(s) to serve both his fellow Christians and non-Christians. The purpose of the gifts is to build up the church (other Christians) (Ephesians 4:12).

The Bible compares the gifts of the Holy Spirit to the parts of the body (1 Corinthians 12). Just as the hands cannot get along without the heart and the nose cannot get along without the mouth, so each spiritual gift depends on the other and works together to complete the whole.

Here is a sample list of the gifts of the Spirit:

teaching	prophecy	giving to others
wisdom	healing	love
evangelism	administration	strong faith
encouragement	knowledge	hospitality
mercy	apostleship	leadership

Some gifts are spectacular. Others are expressed quietly. But no gift makes any person more important. The one gift which is superior is the one which all Christians can have, love.

Check It Out: Read 1 Corinthians 12—13; Ephesians 4:1-13; and Romans 12:4-13 for listings of the gifts and how they are to work together.

The Holy Spirit and Me

The Holy Spirit can have a powerful effect on your life. One of his goals is to draw people to God and help them to understand his truths.

Think about your life for a moment. In what areas are you dissatisfied? How do you think God could make those areas better? The Holy Spirit can help you to discover God's solutions to your problems and frustrations.

Think: If you are a Christian, look back at the list of the "fruit of the Spirit." Write them down. Put a star beside the one that you feel you express most often. Put an arrow beside ones that you need to allow the Holy Spirit to express more fully through you. Beside each one list a situation/person toward whom you can express it. For example, you might need the Holy Spirit's power in being patient with your brother.

5
The Bible: Guide for Living

ooooooooooooooooooooooooooo

"What makes the Bible so special? How is it different from other religious books? Why does it have so much authority over Christians? How can a book that old have any use today?"

The Bible's Unique Characteristics

It Is Inspired

Christians believe that the Bible is uniquely inspired by God. The biblical term *inspired* means "God breathed." God breathed the life and meaning into the Bible's words. God is its author. Because of this, the Bible is intended to have authority over all attitudes and actions. It is relevant to all situations. No other book, religious or otherwise, can make these claims.

Christians believe that God wrote the Bible by guiding human writers to record his truth. Many writers of different times and different occupations wrote the Bible. Even so, the same truth runs throughout. This remarkable unity assures Christians that the Bible is inspired by God and is uniquely qualified to guide their lives.

Check It Out: Read the first four books of the New Testament. Each tells about Jesus' life on earth. What does each writer emphasize? How do they differ? How are they the same?

It Has Authority

Because the Bible is inspired by God, Christians believe that it has authority over the way they live. Christians let the Bible guide them. They measure themselves, other people, ideas, thoughts, and actions by the Bible. If the Bible says to do it, it is right to do. If the Bible says not to do it, it is not right to do. Some of the things the Bible says to do are:

- Express love to other people, even those who hate you
  - Meet the needs of other people even if it costs you
    - Communicate with God (pray)
      - Depend on God for what you need and want
        - Do right instead of just talking about it
          - Be thankful for the good things that happen
            - Rest and worship one day each week
              - Forgive other people
                - Honor your parents
                  - Enjoy living.

Some of the things that the Bible says not to do are:

                  - Put yourself first
                - Depend on money for happiness
              - Murder or otherwise destroy people
            - Insult people
          - Have sex outside of marriage
        - Steal possessions
      - Lie to ourselves or others
    - Want what someone else has
  - Hold grudges
- Get drunk

Check It Out: One biblical list of rights and wrongs is called the Ten Commandments and is found in Exodus 20:3-17. Another list of is found in Colossians 3:5-17.

Speaks to All Subjects

A unique characteristic about the Bible is that it speaks in broad terms to all topics. Even though the Bible was written thousands of years ago, it still applies to current concerns. How? People are the same from generation to generation, and the problems we face are very similar. The details change, but the basic issues do not. For example, we have always been and always will be concerned about relationships with the opposite sex.

Concerns which are not addressed directly are dealt with through guidelines. For example, the Bible does not tell a Christian whom to marry. But it does state that:

- Marriage is good (Genesis 2:18,24; Proverbs 18:22).
- The partner should be a Christian (2 Corinthians 6:14).
- The two should be willing to submit to each other, love each other, and meet each other's needs (Ephesians 5:21-33).
- Marriage is a commitment that should last throughout life (Mark 10:7-9).

Try It Out: The Bible does not tell us exactly who to pick for friends. However, God is very concerned about our friends. What do the following verses say about which friends to choose? Hebrews 10:24; 1 Corinthians 15:33; Proverbs 17:17; 20:6,19; Ecclesiastes 4:9-10; 1 Samuel 16:7.

The Evidences Back It Up

The Bible is special, not just because Christians believe in it but because many types of evidence support it.

- Many of the historical events of the Bible are confirmed by other history books.
- Before the printing press was invented, books had to be copied by hand. Thus potential for mistakes in copying was great. However, there are many copies of the Bible from many different dates and all match extremely well. No other literature has so many matching copies.
- Archaeological discoveries support the locations and events of the Bible.
- The Bible was written by many types of people and in many different styles, yet it agrees. This is a strong evidence called "internal agreement."
- Countless Old Testament prophesies came true in the New Testament. How do we know someone didn't fake the two to get them to agree? We have copies of the Old Testament which have been scientifically dated hundreds of years before the New Testament was written.
- The events in the Bible show that it is not a fake. If the Bible had been made up by religious people, they would not have included heroes with sins and would not have let Jesus get killed. Instead, the

The Bible: Guide for Living 43

Bible is about real people with real failures and real forgiveness.

Check It Out: Read in these passages what the Bible says about itself: 2 Timothy 3:16; Hebrews 1:1; 2 Peter 1:21; John 10:35; Luke 24:44.

What's the Bible About?

The Bible contains God's instructions for living life.

The people in the Bible are people just like you and me. They sometimes made mistakes and sometimes did the right thing. No matter what they did, God continued to work with them and to love them through it all. These people experienced many emotions: joy, depression, love, anger, confusion, and more.

They encountered every kind of experience: loneliness, contentment, confusion, understanding, temptation, success, grief, sickness, discovery, lack of confidence, fear, and adventure.

They felt both near to and far away from God. Some respected and obeyed God, and some did not. They were people with questions and people with answers.

The people in the Bible were not perfect examples of what Christians are supposed to be like. Rather, they were real people who learned in real life how God handles people and situations.

Try It Out: Read about each of the following people. Decide what each can teach you about God. In the column to the right are some suggestions. Read it only after you have come up with your own ideas.

Cain (Genesis 4)	God wants to help us with our anger.
Noah (Genesis 6:9 to 9:17)	Obey God for your own protection.
Esau; Jacob (Genesis 25:27-34)	Think about the long-range consequences.
Joseph (Genesis 37—41)	Life will get better!
Moses (Exodus 3—4)	God will empower you to do what you need to do.
Samaritan woman (John 4)	No matter what you've done, Jesus loves you. Start anew.
Pharisees (Matthew 23:1-7)	Not everybody in church is a Christian.
Peter (Mark 14:27-31,66-72; Matthew 16:18-19)	Even dedicated Christians fail. God uses even people who make mistakes.

How the Bible Is Written:

The truths of the Bible are communicated through several types of literature, and through many different writers.

Types of Literature

Law: The first five books of the Old Testament contain laws by which God directed his people to live. These five books are also called the Pentateuch, meaning "five volumed teaching" of the law.

History: Much of the Bible is written in historical form. The facts are related as they happened. Readers learn from the events and people of the past. The Old Testament historical books tell about God's relationship with people before Christ lived on earth. The Gospels detail the good news of Jesus Christ's life, death, and resurrection. The Book of Acts traces the growth of the early church.

Poetry: The five poem books are also called Wisdom Literature or "experiential literature." Many of the poems in the Bible were written to be sung in worship services. Psalms contain 150 poems/songs which express the complete range of emotions. Proverbs is full of wise sayings. Song of Solomon is a collection of love poems, picturing the relationship between God and his people.

Prophecy: Prophecy in the Bible is both telling the future and telling the present. Biblical prophets spoke for God. At times God's message related to the future. At other times it was a command or an insight about the present. Isaiah 7:14 and 9:6 prophesied the future birth of Jesus Christ. Habakkuk's prophecy (Habakkuk 2:2-4) helped people understand the present triumph of evil people. Revelation tells about the end of the world. The major prophets (much of what they said is recorded), the minor prophets (some of what they said is recorded), and the Book of Revelation are books of prophecy.

Epistles (Letters): Most of the books of the New Testament are letters which were written to new churches or individuals learning to live the Christian life. They address specific concerns or problems which the church/person was facing. Reading these letters helps us understand and apply Christian principles to life.

Old Testament—39 Books

Law	History	Poetry
Genesis	Joshua	Job
Exodus	Judges	Psalms
Leviticus	Ruth	Proverbs
Numbers	1 and 2 Samuel	Ecclesiastes
Deuteronomy	1 and 2 Kings	Song of Solomon
	1 and 2 Chronicles	
	Ezra	
	Nehemiah	
	Esther	

Major Prophets

	Minor Prophets	
Isaiah	Hosea	Nahum
Jeremiah	Joel	Habakkuk
Lamentations	Amos	Zephaniah
Ezekiel	Obadiah	Haggai
Daniel	Jonah	Zechariah
	Micah	Malachi

New Testament—27 Books

Gospels	Epistles (Letters)	
Matthew	Romans	1 and 2 Peter
Mark	1 and 2 Corinthians	1, 2, and 3 John
Luke	Galatians	Jude
John	Ephesians	
	Philippians	
	Colossians	
History	1 and 2 Thessalonians	Prophecy
Acts	1 and 2 Timothy	Revelation
	Titus	
	Philemon	
	Hebrews	
	James	

Who wrote the Bible? The content originated with God. The truths, ideas, and guidelines are his. But several very different people wrote them down. These people were different in personality, life-style, occupation, and temperament. But they were alike in that each had a relationship with God and witnessed his acts. They wrote what God led them to write.

Sometimes you can discover the author of a particular book by checking the summaries that often appear at the beginning of each book or by looking in a Bible dictionary. Here are four of the authors.

Moses: Under God's guidance, Moses led his people away from slavery to the cruel king of Egypt. Moses was not very confident at first and tried to persuade God to ask someone else. Tradition holds that Moses wrote the first five books of the Old Testament.

David: David was a shepherd as a boy and later became king of Israel. He was dedicated to God but participated in many serious wrongs. God was not pleased with David's wrongs and David suffered many unhappy consequences. However, he continually returned to serving God. He wrote many Psalms.

Paul: Paul was a Jew who hated Christians. While on his way to arrest Christians in Damascus, Paul became a Christian. He became one of the most influential teachers in the early church. He wrote many of the New Testament letters (epistles).

Luke: Luke was a medical doctor who researched his material very carefully. He wrote with precision and detail. He wrote the New Testament Books of Luke and Acts.

Check It Out: Read about these authors in: 1 and 2 Samuel; 1 Kings 1—2 (David); Exodus 2—4 (Moses); Acts 9:1-31 (Paul); Luke 1:3-4; Acts 1:1.

Try It Out: The chapter, "The Bible: Finding Your Way Around," can help you apply the above information. Don't miss it!

6
The Bible: Finding Your Way Around

○○○

Finding Your Way Around in the Bible

Many people find it embarrassing to go to a Bible study and not be able to find the passages. They watch other people turn to Bible verses with ease, and they feel lost. Understanding the Bible's structure and how to find your way around in it can help.

The Bible's Structure

The Bible is divided into sixty-six sections called "books." These books are organized into two "testaments." "Testament" means "agreement" or "covenant" between God and people. The first testament or Old Testament contains information about people and their relationship with God *before* the birth of Jesus Christ. The second testament or New Testament contains information which happened *after* the birth of Christ.

The Bible is complete. There will be no more books added.

Each book is divided into "chapters," and each chapter is divided into "verses." The books are referred to by name such as Matthew or Psalms. The chapters and verses are referred to by number.

A part of the Bible is called a "passage," a "Scripture," or a "verse." Such parts can be any length. Passages are identified by listing the book first, the chapter(s) second, and the verse(s) third. In John 3:16-21: *John* is the name of the book; *3* is the number of the chapter; *16-21* are the numbers of the verses.

Locating Passages

Following these steps will make locating passages easier:

Every passage of the Bible has a book name, a chapter number, and a verse number. These three parts make the reference. It will look like this: *Philippians 4:19.*

The book is named first. The number on the left of the colon is the chapter number. The number(s) on the right of the colon are the verse(s). If there is no colon and thus only one number, all the verses in the chapter are included.

1. Find the Book: Picture the Bible as a book of many smaller books. Look in the table of contents at the front of your Bible. The books are listed in the order in which they appear and are separated into the Old and New Testaments. Sometimes they are also listed alphabetically. Find the page number of the book of Philippians and turn to it. (HINT: Philippians is in the New Testament.)

2. Find the Chapter: Notice that the beginning of each chapter is marked with a large number. Chapter 4 is the last chapter in Philippians.

3. Find the Verse: Look in chapter 4 for verse 19. The verses are marked with small numbers that are usually raised above the words something like footnote numbers. Verse 19 contains all the words which follow the number 19 and precede the number 20. Write Philippians 4:19 on a piece of paper.

When you read the Bible regularly, you will become familiar with where the books are and may not need the table of contents. This has happened for people who find passages so quickly.

Try It Out: Using the above three steps find these passages in your Bible: Proverbs 3:5-7; 2 Timothy 3:16; Acts 17:1; Psalm 119:11.

Getting Started

The only way you will fully grow to understand the Bible is to read it for yourself. There are four important guidelines to follow in beginning to read the Bible.

1. Choose a readable translation.
2. Start in the Gospels.
3. Ask questions!
4. Do what the Bible says.

Choose a Readable Translation

The Bible was originally written in Hebrew and Greek, the everyday languages of the people. Would you have any trouble reading these?

Most of us do not read these languages. For that reason the Bible has been translated into our own everyday languages.

There are several English translations to choose from. Each is a little different because our English language changes from time to time. For example, in the 1600s *suffer* meant "allow" rather than "experience pain." Because of these changes, the King James Bible, translated in the 1600s, will not be as easy to read and understand as one made in the 1900s. To read an older translation, you must understand the terms of its day.

Choose a translation which you can understand. The first page of each Bible states what translation it is. Examples of readable translations are: *New International Version* (NIV) and *The Good News Bible* (GNB).

Start in the Gospels

The Bible is not a book that you read from start to finish like a novel. Though it is possible to read it this way, it is usually more profitable to read it one section at a time and certain books before others. You may want to purchase or borrow a Bible study guide designed especially for your age and your level of Bible knowledge.

John, the fourth book of the New Testament, is a good book to read first. It is one of the Gospels. It tells the good news of Jesus Christ. Write down any questions you have and ask a Christian about them. After you read John, try Romans or Colossians. Then read the rest of the New Testament. When reading the Old Testament, try the books of Genesis, Psalms, and Proverbs first.

Ask Questions!

Do not hesitate to ask questions. Understanding the Bible is a lifelong process. Though many Christians understand it well, no Christian understands it totally. Much of its truth is obvious. Other parts take some time and study to understand. This is one reason the Bible is such an adventure. There is always something new to learn.

Some difficulties in understanding the Bible come because certain practices common in Bible times are unfamiliar to us. To understand verses which use these and other examples, we must talk with someone who can explain them or look them up in a Bible dictionary.

Who can answer your questions? The Christian who gave you this book, a Christian you know, a youth minister, a pastor, or a Bible commentary (book) are likely candidates. If the first person you talk to cannot answer your question, do not give up. Ask if he can find the answer or ask someone else. Finding answers to your questions will increase your understanding of God and his people.

Another way to find answers to your questions is to attend Bible studies. Most churches hold Bible studies each Sunday morning prior to worship services. Many Christians have Bible studies in their homes or at school. Ask a Christian you know to take you to a Bible study or tell you where one meets. You may be able to find one especially geared for new Christians or interested searchers.

What About Disagreement?

You may notice that not all Christians interpret the Bible the same way. Each Christian is trying to put into words some very deep truths and do not always agree on how to do this. Even Christians who give their lives to understanding the Bible are not able to explain each part of it. Hopefully the Christians you know will work out their differences of interpretation in a loving manner. Listen to both sides and decide what makes the most sense to you based on your study of the Bible.

Do What the Bible Says

As you read the Bible, do what it says. One of the best things about the Bible is that living by it improves life. God's ways make sense. For example, encouraging your friends rather than criticizing them has positive results (see Hebrews 10:24-25 and Ephesians 4:29).

At first, you will not understand everything the Bible is telling you, but begin to apply what you do understand. You will find plenty of actions and attitudes to start with.

Obeying the Bible is easier when you remember that there are many more "do's" than "don'ts" in the Bible. Also, for every habit or action you are commanded to give up, you receive much more in return (things like better habits, happier life, better friends). Third, know that God cares for you and wants the best for you. Because he made you, he knows best how you can be happy. He lived by his own advice when he lived on earth as the person Jesus Christ.

Check It Out: Read in these passages what the Bible says about itself: 2 Timothy 3:16; Hebrews 1:1; 2 Peter 1:21; John 10:35; Luke 24:44.

7
Church: A Place to Belong

○○○○○○○○○○○○○○○○○○○○○○○○○○○○○○

What image comes to your mind when the word *church* is mentioned? A building made of brick or wood with a cross on top? Many such buildings exist. But for a Christian this is not the church. The church is composed of people who are Christians, not of construction materials. The buildings made of brick and wood are simply the houses in which the church meets.

The Structure of the Church

Sometimes *church* means the "body of Christ" or the "family of God." In this meaning of *church* every Christian is automatically a part of the church.

Sometimes *church* means the groups of Christians who meet in "local churches." These local churches have names such as "First Baptist Church" or "Grace Lutheran Church." A Christian who belongs to "First Baptist Church" is a part of the same "body of Christ" as one who belongs to "Grace Lutheran Church." This is like saying that she belongs to the family of humans but that her last name is "Jones" which connects her to certain humans in a closer way.

Sometimes these local churches are organized into "associations" or "denominations." These groups of churches provide a sense of togetherness and cooperation with the larger church body.

A denomination is a group of churches who hold certain views as more important than others or who emphasize specific Christian truths. Overall, the similarities between denominations are much greater than the differences.

The Church Gathers to Worship

Christians believe that every day is a day to serve God and to worship him. "Worship" is any action or attitude that expresses appreciation and love for God and as such can be expressed daily. But Christians set aside one special day of the week to worship God together.

This day of worship is Sunday. It is chosen because Jesus arose from death on Sunday. Sunday is often called the "Lord's Day" or the "Sabbath" (day of rest). Many businesses and stores close on Sundays in respect for this day, so that people will not have to work on their worship day.

The time of worship is usually morning. Most Christians spend an hour studying the Bible and an hour worshiping together. The Bible study hour is sometimes called Sunday School. Christians gather in age or interest groups to study the Bible together. The teachers of these studies are church members who feel that God has given them the ability to teach.

During the worship hour, Christians gather in a room called a "sanctuary," an "auditorium," or a "chapel." A leader called a "pastor" or "minister" usually guides the worship. During this time Christians worship God in one or more of these ways:

Reading the Bible

Singing songs (often called "hymns")

Praying (talking to God)

Praising (telling God the things they like about him)

Sharing with each other what God has done in their lives (called "testimonies")

Giving money (called "tithes" and "offerings")

Silence (to pray or think about God)

Listening to Bible teaching (a "sermon")

Check It Out: Hebrews 10:24-25 contains a command to gather for worship and fellowship. Some other commands to worship, often called "calls to worship" are: Psalm 100:2-5; Psalm 34:3; Matthew 11:28-29; Isaiah 40:31.

The worship that God is most pleased with is to "do justly, and to love mercy, and to walk humbly with thy God" (Micah 6:8, KJV).

Church: A Place to Belong 53

Two especially important days of worship for Christians are called Christmas and Easter. Christmas, celebrated on December 25, is the day on which the birth of Jesus Christ is remembered. Easter, observed in the spring, is the day on which his resurrection from death is celebrated.

Baptism

Two special acts of worship are baptism and the Lord's Supper. They can, but do not always, take place every week.

Baptism is the celebration which takes place when someone first becomes a Christian. The new believer is immersed in water by the pastor of the church. Going under the water symbolizes dying to self-centered living, and coming out of the water symbolizes living to Jesus-centered living. Baptism is the celebration of new life in Jesus.

Christians are baptized because Jesus was baptized and the Bible commands it. The ceremony can take place in a river, a large tub called a "baptistry," or in any big body of water.

Check It Out: Read Romans 6:3-8 for an explanation of the meaning of baptism.

The Lord's Supper

The Lord's Supper, sometimes called Communion, is patterned after a supper which Jesus shared with his twelve closest followers shortly before he died. It is actually not a supper at all, but it is a symbolic way to remember Jesus. Participators eat a small piece of bread and drink a swallow of grape juice. The bread represents Jesus' body, and the juice symbolizes his blood. Both are symbols of Jesus having given his life for us.

During the Lord's Supper ceremony, Christians pass the bread and juice to each other. Bible verses are read, and prayers are said. It is a quiet time during which Christians remember that Jesus gave his life for people, think about and are sorry for their wrongs (sins), and thank Jesus for his forgiveness. They feel refreshed and united with other Christians when the ceremony is over. Christians worship this way because Jesus asked them to do it in memory of him.

Matthew 26:26-30 gives an account of the supper Jesus had with his disciples. Luke 22:19-20 includes Jesus' command to take the Lord's Supper in remembrance of him.

Try It Out: Attend a worship service and Bible study this Sunday.

Christians Get Together

Christians love to get together. Many Christians gather for worship, Bible study, and prayer on Sunday nights, Wednesday nights, and other times. Besides worship they get together for the following reasons.

Learning: Christians study the Bible regularly. They share experiences in living the Christian life. They teach each other how to solve problems, how to improve dating and family life, how to face crises, and much more. They believe that God has the best advice for living every area of life.

Support: It is often difficult to live as a Christian. Non-Christians often mock or criticize Christians. Also, many actions of society are directly opposed to Christian values. For example, it is more popular to work toward a new car or a wardrobe than to work to improve relationships. Money is more important than people. These pressures make it hard for Christians to stand up for what they believe. They need each other's support.

It is also difficult to live as a Christian because our own selfishness and stubbornness makes us want to not obey God. We would rather do it ourselves. Christians support each other by reminding one another of the benefits of living God's way.

Celebration: Christians celebrate weddings, births, and people becoming Christians. The happy events in life are even more fun when shared (Romans 12:15).

Comfort: Christians comfort each other at funerals, in hospitals, when sick at home, and when confronting problems or crises. The Bible teaches them to "carry one another's burdens" (Galatians 6:2) and to "weep with those who weep" (Romans 12:15).

Reach out: Christians are eager to reach out to people who are not Christians. They become friends with them, show concern for their problems, love them, meet their needs, and help them to understand what being a Christian is all about. This is called "witnessing." Christians hope others will want to join their family. They want them to experience the same benefits.

Have fun: Christians enjoy life and enjoy being together. A few of the things Christians do together are: eat, talk, have picnics, go on trips,

Church: A Place to Belong   55

play ball, skate, listen to music, watch movies, and sing. These gatherings are often called "fellowships."

Names for the Church

The Bible includes many names for the church. These illustrate what the church is like and what it does.

God's people (1 Peter 2:9-10): The church is composed of God's people. They come in different ages, shapes, colors, heights, and weights. They have different interests and abilities. But all have in common their relationship to Jesus Christ. This similarity is stronger than any of the differences.

The Family (Romans 8:15): Every Christian is a child of God. Thus all are related in a spiritual sense. Sometimes they even call each other "Brother Andrews," "Sister Anne," or simply "sister." God is often called "Father." As a family, Christians love, communicate, sometimes quarrel, are all equally important, have an inheritance (Galatians 4:7), and represent Christ.

The Flock (John 10:27-28): Christians are Jesus' "sheep." He is the shepherd who loves, guides, and takes care of his flock. Sheep are customarily thought of as gentle and responsive, yet helpless without someone to care for them. Jesus gave his life for us, his sheep.

The Body of Christ (1 Corinthians 12:27): The church is the "body of Christ." This means that Jesus Christ is the head, the director, and the people are the body parts which carry out his purposes. This does not mean that Christians are mindless robots who blankly carry out commands. Instead, Christians are unique and very essential parts of a vibrant and functioning body. If any Christian fails to do his job properly, the whole church suffers (1 Corinthians 12:12-26).

Branches of the Vine (John 15:1-8): A vine and its branches illustrate the relationship between Jesus and his followers. The branches (Christians) must remain on the vine (Jesus) in order to survive and bear fruit (see the "Holy Spirit: God in Us" chapter for the fruits of the Spirit).

Serving and Sharing

Christians believe that every Christian is responsible to commit a portion of time, abilities, and money to the church. Because Christians are a family and a body, they are dependent upon each other to meet each other's needs (for encouragement, knowledge, help in times of crisis, and more). They are also responsible for reaching out to people outside the church. Such people might need to become Christians, might be hungry, might need friends, or might have other needs.

Time and Abilities

A Christian is willing to give time and talents to listen to a friend's problem, to teach a Bible study, to fix a meal for someone who is sick, to baby-sit, to clean up, to welcome new Christians, to repair the church building, to mow lawns, and more.

The Holy Spirit gives each Christian the fruit of the Spirit and a spiritual gift which enable the Christian to serve even more effectively. The fruit include such qualities as patience and self-control. An example of a gift is "encouragement." A Christian with this gift would have sensitivity to others and the ability to know just what to say or how to act to make others feel confident.

Check It Out: Acts 2:44-47 illustrates the attitude the first Christians had toward meeting each other's needs. First Corinthians 12:12-27 illustrates the way Christians share their talents.

The fruit of the Spirit is listed in Galatians 5:22-23. The gifts are listed in Romans 12:6-8; 1 Corinthians 12; and Ephesians 4:11-13.

Tithing

Most Christians feel that they should contribute at least 10 percent of their money to support the church and its efforts to meet needs. This is called "tithing." In Malachi 3:10 God challenged his people to bring a tithe and promised a blessing in return. Christians believe that the 90 percent left over will be more than enough to meet their needs. It is actually God's money too, and they seek his guidance in spending it.

Check It Out: Read the challenge in Malachi 3:10.

Leviticus 27:30 explains that one tenth belongs to God.

First Corinthians 16:2 speaks of giving a portion of one's income.

Church Leaders

Some Christians feel a special call to give their entire lives to helping other people become Christians and grow in Christ. Often these people obtain special training in the Bible and church leadership. They then give their lives to working with churches or groups of churches. They are called pastors, ministers, evangelists, ministers of education, youth ministers, children's ministers, campus ministers, and other such titles.

These leaders can be especially helpful in guiding the church toward what God wants it to be. They know that Jesus Christ is the head of the church, and they follow his leadership.

It's Not Perfect

What happened the last time you went to church? Were you: Comfortable? Bored? Excited? Confused? Did you feel at home? What did you enjoy? Not enjoy? What were the people like?

You may be saying to yourself that the church you attended wasn't much like the one described in this chapter. Because the church is made up of people, and people are not perfect, no church will be perfect. Each church has its problems and weaknesses. But each church also has its strengths. Find one in which the strengths outweigh the weaknesses.

In any church there will be people who are not Christians. These people may have joined the church because it was "the acceptable thing to do" or because their friends or family joined. Only those who have a relationship with Christ are actually Christians.

In any church, there will be people who are Christians but are not very sincere about living it. Some Christians do not depend on God in all areas of their lives. There will be people who criticize or argue about the things that go on in the church. Some people will refuse to forgive. These people can be very discouraging to be around. But they are a minority.

Most of the Christians you meet will be eager to please God. They constantly look for new ways to serve God and each other. They encourage each other, help each other learn, make each other feel happy, and try to understand each other even when they don't agree. They will forgive each other and continue to love, even when mistakes are made. They are a joy to be around. When you visit or join a church, concentrate on these people. You will see a glimpse of what God intends the church to be. Your church experience will be a happy one.

Check It Out: To find out what God intends the church to be, read: 1 John 3:16-18; 1 Corinthians 13:1-13; Romans 12:3-13; and Ephesians 4:2-16.

8
Christians: Friends of Jesus

○○○○○○○○○○○○○○○○○○○○○○○○○○○○○○○

Diagram of a Christian

How can you tell if a person is a Christian? If you stood next to one, you might look alike and even act alike in some situations. Being a Christian is not being "different" but being what Jesus Christ wants one to be. In some areas that means being very different. In other areas it means being very much like any other person.

One Who Has Found a Friend

Christians have discovered a marvelous friend. Christianity is primarily a relationship with this friend. His name is Jesus Christ. Jesus is a friend who never lets another down. He has plenty of time to listen to every detail of his friends' concerns. He understands problems and has some great ideas on how to solve them. However, he isn't a pushy advice giver. He speaks mainly when asked and always lets a Christian make up his own mind.

One of the reasons Jesus is so understanding is that he has been through all of the experiences we have. He has been hated by others. He has been ridiculed for doing right. He has been rejected when he needed support. He has felt loneliness, anger, emotional pain, physical pain, fatigue, hunger, depression, frustration, excitement, and more. He has encountered success and failure, temptation and trials, feeling far from and near to God.

Christians are like anyone else in that they need friends. They are different in that they have found the perfect friend.

Check It Out: Hebrews 2:17-18 and 4:15-16 speak of Jesus having experienced the same things we have.

Being friends with Jesus Christ is called "having a relationship with

Christ" or "having invited Christ into your life." Christians have made a conscious decision to become friends with Jesus. They cannot be Christians simply by going to church or by having Christian parents. It is each person's own decision.

A relationship with Jesus is like any other human friendship in the following ways.

1. *Communication.* Friends talk about what is important to them. Jesus wants to hear about each detail of his friends' lives. When his friends speak to him, he does not usually respond in a voice they hear. He has done most of his talking in the Bible.

2. *Admiration.* His friends like him, and he likes them.

3. *Time spent together.* Jesus accompanies Christians everywhere they go. Thus Christians choose activities which please him.

4. *Imitation.* Human friends often begin to act and talk like each other. Likewise, friends of Jesus act like him and develop his qualities.

5. *Growth.* Jesus' friends learn from him. They discover how to please him and how to keep from hurting his feelings. They learn from mistakes. He forgives them, and they start again.

6. *Love.* Jesus loves his friends unconditionally. His friends love him more and more as they relate to him.

7. *Loyalty.* Friends are true to each other and stand up for each other in tough situations. Jesus never lets his friends down or deserts them.

The relationship between Jesus and his friends is unique in the following ways.

1. *Obedience.* Friends might like each other's advice, but they don't have an obligation to follow it. The Christian tries to do exactly what Jesus suggests.

2. *Service.* Friends of Jesus want to serve him. Jesus says that doing things for others is one of the best ways to do this. Thus Jesus becomes the motivation for all the good things Christians do for each other.

One Who Believes in Jesus

Being friends with Jesus is often called "believing in him." Christian belief is illustrated by the following example.

A high school student was vacationing with his family at Niagara Falls. A skilled tightrope walker had stretched his rope across the Falls. There was no safety net. Instead of a balancing pole, the tightrope walker used a wheelbarrow. He made it across safely, and the crowd was ecstatic! The tightrope walker asked, "Do you think I can do it again?" The crowd cheered in affirmation! "What do *you* think?" he asked the student. The student agreed with the crowd, "Of course you can do it! You are the best tightrope walker in the whole world!" The man made it across and back with ease. He asked the student again, "Do you think I can make the walk safely once more?" "Yes, yes! You have done it twice before. I believe you can do it again!" "Are you sure?" the tightrope walker pressed. "Of course I'm sure! I believe in you!" "Then get in the wheelbarrow!" the tightrope walker commanded.

Belief (faith) is getting into God's wheelbarrow. Christians trust their total lives to him. They do what he says even when it means putting themselves at risk. They trust God to make them happy. They know God will not dump them out. He will keep them safe.

Check It Out: Read these verses about belief: Acts 16:31; James 2:14-22.

One Who Imitates Christ

Christians try to imitate Jesus. They ask themselves, "What would Jesus do?" or "How would Jesus feel about this if he were standing right here?" The answer to these questions helps them decide the right attitudes and actions to express in their dating lives, their family struggles, their school experiences, their job responsibilities, their friendships, and every part of life.

Some of the truths that Jesus wants people to live by are:

• Each person is a unique and important creation of God and deserves to be treated with respect and love.

• God will not keep us from problems, but he will give us the power and wisdom to handle them.

• God never asks us to do any more than we can do with his help and power.

• Standing up for what is right is worth the temporary suffering that might result.

• Serving is more important than recognition or position.

One Who Communicates with God

Christians communicate with God. This communication is two-way. Christians communicate with God through Bible reading, prayer, and worship. God communicates with them through the Bible and through prayer. (See the chapter "The Christian Life: Growing" for detail on how Jesus answers prayer.)

Many Christians feel that it is important to set aside a part of each day to spend exclusively with God. This is called a "quiet time" or "personal devotion." During this time Christians read the Bible and pray.

Christians also pray throughout the day. This is a way to communicate with God, to seek his guidance and strength, and to thank him for the good things that happen. For example:

"What do you want me to do about this problem?"

"I don't know what to say to her. I don't know what it feels like to lose my dad in a car accident. Please give me words."

"Help me to be a good sport in this football game."

"Thanks for helping me resist the temptation to cheat!"

"I'm so excited about my date Saturday!"

Check It Out: These verses speak of communicating with God: Mark 1:35; Psalm 34:4; Matthew 11:29; John 15:5-8; Hebrews 4:16; Philippians 4:6-7.

One Who Worships

Christians get together to worship God on Sunday mornings and at other times. Most of these gatherings take place at churches and are called "worship services." They include singing, Bible reading, praying, a talk (sermon) by a minister, giving of money, and sharing of ideas/blessings/needs. Worship services can also take place in a park, a home, or any setting.

Worship services are important to Christians because they need the encouragement of each other, the advice of God's Word, and the joy of expressing their love for God. (See the "Church: A Place to Belong" chapter for more information on why Christians get together and worship.)

Christians also worship God by the way they live their lives. Friends of Jesus know that the way they live brings attention to God. They want to bring him good attention.

Check It Out: Hebrews 10:24-25 encourages Christians to get together. Micah 6:6-8 lists actions which worship God.

One Who Tries to Do What God Wants Him to Do

"How shall I treat my friends?"

"What do I do when I am upset with someone?"

"How do I handle these feelings I'm having?"

Solving their problems the way God wants them to is a daily concern for Christians. This is called "trying to follow God's will." Christians know that they will be happy only when they are doing as God directs. They practice, obeying God daily in such matters as making friends. It will be easier then to understand his will in larger more complex issues, such as who to marry. They discover most of God's will in the Bible. (The chapters on the Bible explain how it speaks to situations.)

Christians try to let God decide how they should spend their time, talents, and money. This is called "stewardship." They see themselves as "stewards" or "those who are responsible for using God's gifts." Letting God guide the way they use their possessions and time is a way friends of Jesus show their confidence in God's advice.

Check It Out: Such verses as Proverbs 3:5-6 give Christians confidence that God will help them to know what to do.

One Who Serves People

Friends of Jesus show their love for him by serving other people. They feel it is their responsibility to express love to people through meeting the emotional, physical, social, and spiritual needs around them. Examples of the ways Christians serve are: listening, teaching, taking care of children, cooking, cleaning, encouraging, counseling, lawn mowing, working with the deaf or otherwise handicapped, visiting prisoners, training new Christians, and visiting lonely or sick people. Such services or "ministries" bring as much joy to the Christian performing them as to the one receiving them.

Check It Out: First Corinthians 13:4-7 describes Christian love. Ephesians 4:2-6,16 encourages Christians to work together, each doing his or her part to accomplish God's work. Matthew 25:31-46 and James 1:26-27 describe Christian service.

One with Temptations and Problems

Christians do not necessarily have life easy. They face temptations and problems just like anyone else. The difference is that they have the power to deal with them. This power comes from God.

Christians continue to face temptation for two reasons:

1. They are still attracted by wrong. Even after becoming a Chris-

tian, our human nature remains. Part of this nature is to want to be involved in wrong (see Romans 7:15 to 8:2).

2. The stronger they become as Christians, the harder Satan (the devil) tries to pull them away from God. They fight temptation by:

—Depending on God's power;

—Knowing what tempts them and avoiding it as much as possible;

—Recognizing the ways Satan tempts and confronting his schemes. ("The Christian Life: Growing" chapter gives more detailed information on temptation.)

Most Christians realize that God does not erase all their problems. Though he helps them avoid certain ones, they experience other problems just like anyone else. Rather than keeping them from problems, God gives the strength to fight them.

Some of the problems that can be avoided by obeying God are:

• Health problems that arise from worry and from not taking care of oneself (smoking, drinking alcohol, using drugs, and so forth)

• Problems arising from doing wrong, such as jail, suspended license, staying after school, venereal diseases.

• Dating and friendship problems that arise from not treating each other with love and respect.

Some of the problems Christians experience like everyone else are:
• Romance problems
  • Illness
    • Friendship problems
      • Tragedy (death, natural disasters, crime)
        • Homework problems and other school problems
          • Problems with parents and siblings
            • Problems with jobs and bosses

Christians believe that if every person lived exactly as God wanted him to live, most of these problems would disappear. But because even Christians don't always live as God desires, problems occur.

Jesus' power makes it easier for Christians to handle problems. For example, being rejected by a friend can be much less devastating to a Christian because Jesus helps him to understand the reasons for the rejection, gives him other friends, and often helps him to be restored to the rejecting friend.

Check It Out: First Corinthians 10:13 explains that God never gives a Christian more temptation or problems than she can handle.

One Who Sometimes Doubts

Christians struggle with doubt. They have doubts about whether God really loves them, about whether the Christian life is worth it, and even about whether God exists. Some Christians fear that doubts show them to be weak or that they are losing their faith. On the contrary, doubt can motivate Christians to grow stronger and can deepen their faith. This happens when Christians are challenged to find the answer to their doubts. (See "The Christian Life: Growing" chapter for some of the ways Christians deal with doubts.)

One Who Keeps On Growing

"Why do Christians sometimes do the same wrong stuff and act just as bad as the rest of us? I don't see why I should be one if they act so much the same."

Christians aren't perfect. They are just forgiven.

Christians believe that when they first accept Jesus, they are like newborn babies (see 1 Peter 2:2-3). They have been born into a whole new kind of life and need a great amount of guidance and help from the Bible and more mature Christians. They continue to make mistakes as they learn.

As Christians grow they understand more of how to live as a Christian, where to go for strength and for answers to questions, how to serve, and how to communicate faith to others. But all Christians still give in to temptations, still misunderstand, still cause problems instead of helping to solve them. Christians don't like this about themselves, and it discourages them.

Check It Out: Romans 7:15 to 8:2 describes the Christian's battle between doing good and doing evil.

One Who Dies but Will Live Again

Christians get sick, suffer, and die just like other people. The difference is: they know that at the end of all the troubles, Jesus has prepared a pain-free life with only pleasure that will last forever. This life takes place in heaven.

What is heaven like? It is probably as different from life on earth as life on earth is different from life before birth.

Imagine that you are an unborn baby: All you know is life in a watery, dark, confined place. The sounds of your mother's body are consistent and comforting. Temperature is constant. Life is predictable. If we could communicate with you, how would we explain such concepts as dryness, light, breathing air, hugging people, seasons, and colors?

Taking the illustration further, a baby has to go through a great deal of pressure and pain to enter the world outside its mother. But the freedom and new experiences on the outside make the pain worth it. Likewise death and the events leading up to it may not be much fun. But knowing that heaven awaits on the other side makes the journey through death more bearable.

Check It Out: First Corinthians 15:51-55 teaches about life after death and that death's sting is taken away. First Thessalonians 4:13-18 explains that the Christian grieves but with hope.

One Who Shares His Faith with Others

Christians feel that they have found a good thing. They want others to meet and get to know their friend Jesus. They feel that their happiness, strength, and enjoyment of life comes from him. It is no surprise that they would want to share this with other people. This is called "witnessing."

Christians witness in three ways:

1. *What God through Christ has done for everyone:* Christians share Bible verses which explain that God loves us and has provided a way for us to be reunited with him. The "Roman Road" is one set of verses. It is called this because the verses are all from Romans and they are steps on the "road to salvation." Read them in order: Romans 3:23; Romans 6:23; Romans 5:8; Romans 10:9-10; Romans 8:1; and Romans 12:1-2.

2. *What God has done for them:* This is called a "testimony." Christians are excited about what God has done and is doing in their own lives. They feel that if you know about what he has done for them, you will want him to do similar things for you.

A sample testimony is: "Before I met Jesus, I got very depressed whenever I had a problem. I felt powerless to change things. I had heard that Jesus was interested in problems, so I decided to try him. When Jesus entered my life, he showed me that he cares about the details of my life. He helps me find solutions to my problems. I still get depressed; but because Jesus helps me understand and fight my depression, it is not nearly as severe, or as long."

3. *What God plans for the future:* Friends of Jesus believe that he has good things in store for their personal future. They know God has a purpose for the events which happen and that God will take care of them no matter what happens.

Christians also believe that Christ is coming back to take them to live with him forever. This forever life will have none of the problems of this world. This return of Jesus is called the second coming.

Christians may approach you to share with you in any of the above three ways. Some Christians come on strong, and this may be difficult for you. Try saying something like, "Whoa! You are coming on a little strong for me." Most Christians will understand and relax. Often they are as nervous sharing with you as you are for them to share with you. Their faith is so important that it is hard for them to talk about it in a relaxed way.

Learn all you can and be open to the good news they share with you. It can change your life.

Summary

A Christian is one who:
    Is a friend of Jesus Christ;
      Tries to be like Jesus in words, actions, attitudes;
        Communicates with Jesus;
          Tries to do God's will;
            Loves and serves people;
              Has power to handle temptations and problems;
                Struggles with doubts;
                  Is still growing;
                    Will live forever;
                      Shares his faith with others.

Think: How are Christians different from other people? How are they the same?

How would I benefit by becoming a Christian or by growing as a Christian?

What keeps me from becoming a Christian? How can the benefits outweigh my hesitation?

9
God's Family: You Can Join

○○○○○○○○○○○○○○○○○○○○○○○○○○○○○○○○○

You Can Join God's Family

"This Christianity stuff sounds interesting. I think I might like to try it. I have some misgivings though. I really don't know if I'll like it. I'm not even sure what I am getting into."

Getting Started

Becoming a Christian is like getting married. A man gets to know someone, decides that he wants to spend his life with her, gets married, and then spends the rest of his life learning how to be married. He constantly learns more about his wife and grows in relationship to her. He learns how to please her, how to let her know his needs, and how to become one with her.

Likewise, a person who decides to become a Christian learns about Christianity, commits himself to God through the person Jesus Christ, and then spends the rest of life learning how to live out his new relationship with God. This is called being a "disciple" or learner. Disciples learn from Jesus how to live.

Both marriage and Christianity are adventures in living. Often they are exciting and exhilarating. Sometimes they are difficult, confusing, or frustrating. Always there are opportunities to grow, to discover, to enjoy. Neither is a stagnant relationship. Both are either growing or falling apart.

How does one join God's family? It helps to understand a little of what being a Christian is. Like marriage, you never fully understand it until you actually enter the relationship, but you can learn a lot about what you are getting into. This chapter and the previous chapters of this book should help.

Becoming a Christian is giving God control of your life. This is *"repentance."* The first part of repentance is to realize that living life without God is pointless and not as much fun as you once thought. You feel sorry for having lived your own way. The second part of *repentance* is to decide to change over completely to God's side. One who "repents" changes from living one's own life to living God's life.

Changing to living God's life does not mean to change everything. Rather, it means to change the things God wants you to change. For example, if you found it easy to make friends as a non-Christian, you would keep that same positive quality. But a characteristic such as always wanting your own way would be changed to considering the needs of others.

Becoming a Christian means to *begin again.* One leaves the pain and mistakes of the past behind and begins on a new adventure. None of us is good enough to be a Christian. God knows this, forgives us, and gives us a fresh start. This new beginning is described as a "new birth" in John 3:1-8.

Being a Christian means *living a new kind of life* which lasts forever. It is a life lived in contact with God. This means that we try to think God's thoughts and do what God wants.

Being a Christian means that *God meets all of our needs.* Sometimes he does this through our own efforts. (We work at a job to buy clothes.) Other times he does it through the efforts of others. (Friends help us by listening to our problems.) Still other times he does it directly himself. (He gives us a feeling of peace during a difficult test.)

Being a Christian means *being a member of God's family.* This family is made up of all Christians everywhere. Groups of this family meet, worship, and serve together in churches (See the chapter "Church: A Place to Belong"). When one Christian meets someone else who is a Christian, they automatically have something in common.

According to Youth

Here are some quotes from Christian youth, expressing why they are Christians:

"He [Jesus] is my close friend. I can talk to him, and he gives me advice and helps me. I had a really low self-image and was afraid to step out. Jesus said he'd help me, and he does."

"I think I am more caring and loving. I have more friends."

"Some of my friends think I'm crazy for being a Christian, so I'm not always popular. But I'm more happy and content."

"At some points I feel so close to him that I can't feel lonely. I know he cares and that he would never harm me. He gives me strength and fills my empty spots. The neatest part is knowing that he understands me, both the good and bad parts and accepts me as I am. I'm not perfect and am ashamed of some of the things I do, but God is working to fix me up."

"I don't think I could work through my problems without God. Also, I want to live forever."

"A Christian is a loving person who is concerned with other people's problems and tries to be an example of what Jesus is like. I want to be like that."

"I am a Christian because I enjoy being with Christians. A Christian is someone you can talk to, someone who can keep secrets and problems within themselves, someone to trust."

"God helps you get through school, like during a hard test."

"Being a Christian makes you more careful and aware of what you and other people say and do."

"The best thing about being a Christian is knowing that God is always there when I need him."

Accepting Jesus

Being a Christian is to accept Jesus Christ. This means to trust him as Savior, Lord, and Friend.

Savior

We trust him as Savior because he "saves" us *from* life without God and *to* life with him. Everyone sins (does wrong or fails to do right). The consequence of such wrong actions is death and eternal separation from God. Separation from God yields eternal unhappiness, frustration, loneliness, and restlessness. After physical death, those who choose to remain separated from God go to hell, a place of misery and aloneness.

Because of Jesus, we can be saved from these consequences. When we accept him, we are reunited with God and receive eternal life instead of eternal death. Eternal life does not start at death. It begins the minute one becomes a Christian. Earthly life is characterized by peace, power to solve problems, satisfaction, and enjoyment. Life after death is in heaven, a delightful place of unity with God and other Christians.

Check It Out: Titus 2:11-14 describes some of the things Jesus saves us from and to.

Lord

We trust him as Lord because he becomes our Master. We allow Jesus to guide us and tell us how to live. Most of the things he wants us to do are written in the Bible. Normally, we don't like anyone to tell us what to do, but because we believe that Jesus knows better than we do and that he has our best interests in mind, we let him be our boss. Also Jesus never asks us to do anything without helping us to do it.

Check It Out: Matthew 11:28-30 describes the loving and restful way Jesus deals with people.

Friend

We trust him as Friend because he has all the qualities of a good friend, and none of the shortcomings. He is always ready to listen to our problems. His advice always works. He sees the good in us. He is constantly there to encourage us. He understands our problems because he has been through the same ones.

Check It Out: Hebrews 2:17-18 and 4:15-16 explain that Jesus has been through it all. He can sympathize and offer useful advice in dealing with every situation.

Enter the Relationship

Once you understand some of what becoming a Christian means, you may want to take steps toward entering the relationship.

1. *Realize your need for God.* First of all realize that you need God. Understand that you are out of touch with him and that you have made him unhappy by disobeying him (sinning). Know that only God can make your life happy.

Hint: Some folk are murderers and skid row bums. Others are simply self-centered and cheat in school. Still others are basically good. But none matches God's perfect standard. Sin means "missing the mark." Picture an archery target. The first arrow comes within an inch of the bull's eye. The second comes within three inches. The third arrow misses the target completely. The first arrow was the closest, but it still cannot qualify as a bull's eye. Similarly, all sins miss what God intends for us to be and do.

2. *Know that Jesus is the way to God.* Second, come to understand that Jesus lived, died, and rose from death (resurrected) so that you could personally be reunited with God. This is called the "atonement." Dividing the word up helps us understand its meaning: at-one-ment. We can be "at one" or united with God because of Jesus. "Christ died for sins once and for all, . . . in order to lead you to God" (1 Peter 3:18).

3. *Personally accept Jesus.* Each person must decide whether or not to accept Jesus as Savior, Lord, and Friend. Not to decide is to decide against him. Revelation 3:20 states that Jesus is knocking on the door of our lives, waiting to be let in. Only you can decide to open the door. To open the door and accept Jesus, pray (talk to Jesus), saying something like:

"Jesus, I'm sorry that I have ignored you for so long. I realize now that living life my way just won't do. Please forgive me. I'd like to give you my life and live for you. Will you come into my life and make me into what you want me to be? Help me to know how to live for you."

Know that he has come into your life as he stated in John 6:37: "I will never turn away anyone who comes to me." Once you have told Jesus your desire to live with him, you are a Christian. God lives in your life and has already begun to direct, comfort, and encourage you.

4. *Tell other Christians about it.* It is very important that you tell other Christians about your decision to become a Christian. When other Christians know about your decision, they can give you the encouragement and guidance you need. Also, telling others helps your decision become more real to you.

Try to tell one Christian right away. This might be the pastor of your church or the person who told you about Jesus.

As soon as possible, tell the church. This is called making a "public profession of faith" or "public decision." Many churches offer a time of commitment at the end of the worship service. This is called an "invitation." During the invitation song, walk to the front and tell the pastor about your becoming a Christian. You may have become a Christian at that very moment or at an earlier time. Some pastors ask the new Christian to tell the church about the decision. Others do it for them.

As a new Christian, the church will welcome you into its family. The Christians in the church are always very excited when someone becomes a Christian. God and his angels have a celebration each time a person becomes a Christian (Luke 15:10)!

You will also be baptized. Baptism is a ceremony during which you are immersed in water to symbolize your death to self-centeredness and birth to new life in Christ.

5. Begin to *live the Christian life*. You can find out what God wants you to do by reading the Bible, by going to church, and by observing other Christians.

Check It Out: Read about baptism in Romans 6:1-8.

Growing as a Christian

After establishing this initial relationship with God through Jesus, begin to let him change your life. Some of the steps toward growth are:

1. Read the Bible to learn about God and to find out what he wants you to do (2 Timothy 3:16). You are now a "disciple" of Christ. A disciple is one who learns. As you live out what he teaches you, your faith will become more firm and will make more sense.

2. Pray (talk to God) to get to know God better and to open yourself up to what he wants you to do and be (Mark 1:35).

3. Begin to do things as God wants you to. You won't understand everything immediately, but you will find plenty that you do understand (John 14:21).

4. Turn away from self-centeredness. A common formula for *joy* is to spell it out—*J*esus first, *O*thers second; and *Y*ourself third.

5. Join a church and find ways to serve Christ through it. Through the people of the church you can learn, worship, and serve (Hebrews 10:24-25). Serve your church by giving part of your income (Malachi 3:10) and part of your time (Romans 12:6-8).

6. Live out your faith in your daily activities (1 John 3:18). Look for people in your routine—at school, job, and home—whom you can serve. Some ideas are: listen to problems, help with homework, invite someone to join you for lunch, smile, tell about your new relationship with God.

7. Find and hang around Christian friends. You will find many of these at your church. Be sure to find them at school and in the other places you go. Their example and encouragement will be invaluable to

God's Family: You Can Join 73

you (1 Corinthians 15:33 and Hebrews 10:25).

8. Tell other people about what being a Christian means to you. This is called "witnessing" or "giving your testimony" and can help others become interested in Christianity (Matthew 28:19-20).

Understand What You Have

As mentioned above, Christians spend their whole lives learning what it means to be a Christian. There is always more to learn which adds to the adventure of life with Christ. The best source of information is the Bible. Christian books can also be helpful. The last chapter in this book can help you to understand some of the words of the Christian faith.

Briefly, you have as a Christian:

Salvation: You are saved *from* separation from God and saved *to* a relationship with him. You are saved from eternal misery and to eternal enjoyment.

Relationship: You have a personal relationship with God. This means that you are able to communicate with God, spend time with him, and become like him. He is your best friend and the source of meeting your needs. He gives you the information and guidance you need to live a happy life.

Power: You have God's power available to you. When you allow it to work, it will help you to solve your problems, to make the right decisions, to resist temptation, and to live the Christian life. It is stronger than any other power that exists.

Family: You have a new parent (God), new brothers and sisters (Christians), and a new inheritance (life with God complete with the meeting of all your needs). You will grow to depend on each other, to work out problems, to meet each other's needs, to enjoy being together, and to understand each other.

Check It Out: 1 Peter 2:9-10 lists titles for Christians.

Uphold Your Covenant

A covenant is an agreement between two persons. Each promises to do certain things for the other. Each pledges to uphold the commitment to the other. Becoming a Christian is making a covenant with God. In your covenant with God you have responsibilities toward him,

74 Getting to Know God

and he has responsibilities toward you.

God will ask you to:	*You can ask God to:*	*Reference*
Learn and live his ways	Teach you his ways	Matthew 11:29-30
Confess your sins	Cleanse you from sin	1 John 1:9
Resist temptation	Give you the power to resist temptation	1 Corinthians 10:12-13
Change your life-style	Offer ideas and power	Romans 12:1-2
Tell others about him	Give you words to say and courage to say them	Matthew 28:18-20 Matthew 10:19-20

The Place of Feelings

You may have noticed the good feeling that a relationship with Christ can bring. Especially when one first becomes a Christian, there is often a flood of happy emotion.

But the feelings fade. A Christian may find himself wondering what happened. "Did God leave me?" "What did I do wrong?" "Where are the good feelings?" Feelings, though nice, are not the proof of one's relationship with God. Rather, God's promises to us (in the Bible) are the foundation and proof of our relationship with him. A well-known illustration pictures one's Christian life as a train.

Faith: The engine or facts pulls the train and gives it its power. These facts are found in the Bible. Some of these are: God loves us; God forgives us when we ask; God will stay with us forever; We will not be disappointed by life with him.

Facts: We attach our faith to the facts. The faith is the "fuel car." It gives the facts power. Because we have faith (trust) in the facts, we are willing to live by them.

Feelings: The train can run with or without the caboose (feelings). Feelings are an enjoyable addition but not essential to the running of the train. Sometimes we feel great. Other times we feel rotten. Our relationship with Christ is secure either way.

I Still Don't Know

So you still aren't sure whether you want to become a Christian? You are not alone. Many people approach Christianity with caution and skepticism.

God's Family: You Can Join   75

Try this: Have the courage to investigate Christ and his claims. Read the Bible. Get to know some Christians. Attend some Bible studies. Pray something like:

"God, I'm not even sure that you exist. But if you do and if you can hear this prayer, I want you to know that I am open to learning about you. Show me the truth. Help me to know if you are real and what a relationship with you means. Help me to have the courage to accept Jesus Christ and to live for you."

You have much to gain through becoming a Christian. Try it! You won't be disappointed.

Check It Out: Read the Book of Romans for a summary of what Christians believe about God and themselves. Matthew 5—7 is a concise account of Jesus' teachings.

10
The Christian Life: Growing

ooooooooooooooooooooooooooooo

"Once I've become a Christian, what do I do?"

Basic information on growing as a Christian is included in other chapters of this book. Here we'll explore in greater depth some of the ways Christians grow:

- A daily time with Christ
  - Prayer
    - God's will
      - Resisting temptation
        - Dealing with doubt
          - Stewardship and service
            - Obedience

Daily Quiet Time

Setting aside a part of each day to spend exclusively with God can help you understand him better, help you know how to live the Christian life, and give you the power to live it. Christians call this time a "quiet time" or a "personal devotion." During this time Christians read the Bible and pray. They ask God to help them understand the Bible verses they read, share concerns and pleasures with God, and seek his guidance for the day.

Some Christians have their quiet time in the morning. Others have it at lunch or at night before going to sleep. Fifteen minutes a day is a good amount of time to begin with. Some Christians use guidebooks to help them decide what to read, pray, and think about.

Steps toward establishing a quiet time are:

1. Set a definite time and keep it. Even if you spend only five

minutes at first, do your quiet time consistently.

2. Find a place where you will be undisturbed and can concentrate. Your bedroom or a private spot in your house are fine.

3. Decide a plan. Purchase a devotional guide or devise your own plan for Bible reading and prayer. Perhaps you will read a chapter of the New Testament each day and pray for three minutes.

4. Keep on keeping on. Ask for help if you become discouraged. Let it become a habit you cannot live without.

Try It Out: Here is a sample guide for a quiet time. Follow these directions to have your own quiet time:

1. Read 1 Peter 5:6-7.

2. List on a piece of paper all the things you worry about.

3. Thank Jesus that he cares about your worries. Read 1 Peter 5:7 again, substituting your list for the word *cares* or *anxieties*.

4. Choose one of the worries. What do you think Jesus wants you to do to solve it? How do you think he will help you with it?

Prayer

Prayer is talking with God. Just as you talk to your friends to get to know them and to continue to understand them, prayer helps you and God draw close and remain close.

Through prayer you can:
- Tell God what you like about him
- Find strength to handle problems
- Ask his advice
- Understand the Bible better

During prayer God helps you to:
- Know what to say
- Understand God's ways
- Know how to act
- Become more like Jesus

Christians pray when alone, while in groups, and even when in the middle of conversations with other people. Be sure to talk in your words just as you would to any friend. *Thees, thous,* and other churchy words aren't at all necessary or even helpful.

Prayer is not always easy. Here are two possible problems.

Why Do My Prayers Go Unanswered?

"Does God hear my prayers? I feel like they just bounce back. Why doesn't he seem to answer me?"

Prayer is difficult for many Christians. Understanding the way God answers can help. He always answers prayer, but not always with yes. His answer can also be no or wait. In addition, his answer might change the person praying rather than the circumstances. Here are some examples:

"Lord, please make my parents easier to get along with! They are driving me crazy!"

God might say yes to this prayer by helping the Christian to see places he can work to improve the relationship. In this way God changes the son, rather than the parents. But the results are the same: The relationship improves. God might also guide the parents to be understanding, which would doubly improve the relationship.

"God, I am so lonely. I know you have created me to need a partner in my life. Please send me the man you have for me."

When no dates come after six months, it seems as though God has ignored this girl's request. But, God might be answering wait. He is preparing the girl and her future boyfriend, helping both to develop a wide range of relationships with friends of both sexes. This would give each of them the skills necessary for a good romance and a strong relationship. Two years later, they may meet. But if she becomes impatient and tries to push a relationship with someone she doesn't really like just to have a boyfriend, she may end up with less than God's best. It is better to wait for a steak than to settle for a hamburger.

"God, I want a car. It is really hard to get around in a city this size without one. I have Bible studies to attend, practice after school, and errands to run. Besides, I would like to date without having to always ask for my parents' car."

God might answer no to this person. God knows that the expense of the car would not leave enough money for clothes, dates, fun money, college savings, giving to the church, and other needs. God would help the person to understand that he wants him to enjoy his high school years and not be tied down to an expense he can do without.

When we try to work against God's answers, problems result. God can see the future and guides us toward what would make us truly happy. His advice guards us against circumstances that would be destructive to us. We might feel that another path is better, but God really does know more than we do. The more we work to accept and obey the answers he gives, the happier we are.

"God has never talked to me. How can I understand what he wants me to do if he won't tell me?"

It is true that God does not usually speak in an audible voice, but he does communicate. He speaks in the following ways.

1. *The Bible:* Most of what God wants us to do has already been communicated in the Bible.

2. *Jesus Christ:* God has shown us how to live by live demonstration. He lived the perfect human life through the person Jesus Christ.

3. *Christian common sense:* A feeling that something is right based on prayer and the Bible is often God communicating.

4. *More mature Christians:* If other Christians think an action or attitude is a good idea, it often is.

5. *Circumstances:* God can work through circumstances by causing certain things to happen or not happen.

God's Will

Christians are eager to do what God wants them to do because they know he is best able to make them happy. Each time you obey God your understanding and enjoyment of what he wants for you will grow.

Often God's will is the same as the Christian's will. But when it differs, Christians try to do what God suggests because he knows more about the situation and about what will happen in the future. Christians often end their prayers with "if it be your will." This means that they want the answer to the prayer to be yes only if God thinks it is a good idea.

Check It Out: Such verses as Proverbs 3:5-6 give Christians confidence that God will help them to know what to do.

Try It Out: Answer these questions when trying to decide God's will:
Is it good for me? (1 Corinthians 6:12).
How will it affect others? (1 Corinthians 10:23-33).
How would life be if everyone did this?
Do I want others to know I am doing it?
Does the Bible say to do it or not do it? (John 14:21).
What do other Christians say about it? (Proverbs 11:14).
Am I willing to obey even if I don't like God's answer? (James 1:5-6).
Does it bring attention to God? (1 Corinthians 10:31; Colossians 3:23).

Resisting Temptation

"I am a Christian. I know it is wrong to drink, but I do it anyway. No matter how hard I try to resist, I end up giving in eventually. I have heard that when I ask forgiveness, God will give me the strength to resist the next time. I do feel his power, but it doesn't seem strong enough."

All Christians struggle with temptation. Most of them have an area in which they sin repeatedly. They feel powerless to stop. The battle is not an easy one, but it can be won through God's power. The struggle comes from two forces:

1. Even though Christians have been "born again" into a new life, they still have part of their old life that urges them to do wrong. This is called "sinful nature."

2. An evil being called the devil or Satan works constantly to draw Christians away from God. He makes our sinful nature even harder to resist.

Though it is not bad to be tempted, it is bad to give in to temptation. Even so, every person yields to temptation occasionally. Christians find forgiveness and cleansing when they tell God about the wrong they have done. Unfortunately, the consequences of the sin (wrong) often remain. For example, sex outside of marriage might result in pregnancy or venereal disease. Although the Christian can be forgiven for the activity, the baby or disease remains. For this reason, Christians believe that it is better not to sin in the first place.

Some temptations that young Christians face are:
Wanting friends so badly that I would do anything to get them;
Not living like a Christian because people may not like me;
Cheating on my boyfriend or girl friend;
Wanting or taking someone or something that is not yours;
Drinking and/or drugs.

Three ways Christians resist temptation are:
1. Realize the power it has over them and try to avoid situations in which they will be faced with the temptation. When they must face it, they ask other Christians to pray for them.

2. Understand that the battle against temptation is a normal, but not fun, part of the Christian life. As they learn to use God's power, they give in less and less.

3. Learn the nature of the devil, the schemes he uses, and ways to recognize and resist the schemes:

Though typically thought of in a red suit with a pitchfork and pointy tail, the devil appears in whatever form is most attractive. For example, he may tempt a dieter through a hot fudge sundae. He might tempt a lonely person through an unhealthy dating relationship.

Satan uses tactics like these:

He shows you what is attractive about the sin: "Doesn't that hot fudge sundae look great! Who cares if you're on a diet—you deserve some really good food once in awhile!"

He "forgets" to tell you the bad things that can result from giving in to a temptation: "Go ahead and quit school. You can get paid for working. You aren't getting paid for going to school!" The devil doesn't mention that jobs without a diploma often pay less and are even more boring than school.

He tells only part of the truth: "You know that God intends for men and women to enjoy each other. Why wouldn't he want you to express your love through sex?" It's true that God made sex to enjoy, but he made it for use within marriage. The devil doesn't mention the problems which occur otherwise.

He tells you the sin will make you happy, even when it won't: You sure will feel better if you cheat. An *A* is much better than a *D*. You'll be happy, and your parents will be happier." The devil doesn't admit that cheating causes pain, too.

He concentrates on short-range benefits: "Why wait? You know you want that car. So what if it will cost more in interest buying it now than waiting till you have the money saved. You can worry about that later. Life is short. Enjoy it!"

He speaks for God, but seldom says what God would say: "God will understand if you do it just once. It won't make that much difference . . . " It *does* make a difference.

These are some ways Christians resist Satan's schemes:

1. *Know the truth:* Knowing the truth makes it easier to spot Satan's lies. For example: "I know sex will be even better if I wait till marriage."

2. *Read the Bible:* The Bible is the best source for discovering the truth. In addition, there are many instances of people who were tempted. Learn from the ways they reacted.

3. *Avoid tempting situations:* Know what tempts you and stay away from it when possible. For example, it is easier to keep from eating chocolate sundaes if there is no ice cream in the house.

4. *Hang around with Christians:* If others are trying to resist temptation, it becomes easier for you to do so.

5. *Talk to friends:* When you feel temptation coming on or know you will be in a tempting situation, talk to Christians who will give you support and pray for strength for you. Ask how they handle the particular temptation you are facing.

6. *Depend on God's power:* Though Satan is strong, God is stronger. God always provides a way to resist temptation.

7. *Realize that it is much easier to resist temptation than to undo the consequences of giving into it.* It is better to keep from saying harmful words than to try to take them back.

Check It Out: Romans 7:15 to 8:2 illustrates the Christian's struggle with temptation. First John 1:9 tells about God's forgiveness. First Corinthians 10:13 and Philippians 4:13 assure Christians they will never face a temptation too strong for them.

Dealing with Doubt

All Christians struggle with doubt at one time or another. Doubts do not mean you are weak, or that you are losing your faith. On the contrary, doubt can motivate you to grow stronger and can deepen your faith. This happens when you accept the challenge to find the answer to the doubt.

An example: a Christian who worries that Jesus has left her may simply be relying too heavily on feelings. Discovering that Jesus' love is consistent and not dependent on feelings can help this Christian to be more confident of God's love in the future.

Some of the ways Christians deal with doubts are:

—Tell God how they are feeling.

—Try to discover the source of the doubt.

—Study Bible passages explaining the doubt or telling how a Bible character dealt with the doubt.

—Read articles or books about how other Christians have dealt with that area of doubt.

—Talk with more mature Christians about how they would handle the doubt.

—Give the doubt a little time to settle.

—Find evidence for or information about the doubted fact.

Check It Out: One of the disciples, sometimes called Doubting Thomas, doubted whether the risen Jesus Christ was really Christ himself. Jesus did not criticize Thomas or the other disciples that doubted. Rather, he offered the evidence of his nail-scarred hands. Read about this in John 20:24-29.

Stewardship and Service

Everything that you have, all you can do, and all you hope to do are possible ways to serve God. Consulting him about how to use your time, talents, possessions, and activities is a way to show your respect for his wisdom and advice. Doing what he says is called "stewardship." You are the "steward" or manager of what God has given you. Following his advice will help each area of your life grow to be the happiest it can be.

An important habit to cultivate is called "tithing." To tithe is to give 10 percent of your money to the church. The money is used to help others learn about God. It is easiest to begin tithing when you do not have much income. Then as your income grows, it is natural to continue the process. Tithing helps you grow by putting God first in financial matters and trusting him to meet your monetary needs.

Check It Out: God challenges Christians to tithe in Malachi 3:10. He promises blessings as a result.

Try It Out: List the things you do each day. How do these please or fail to please God? What changes would he advise?

Write down the things you like to do and the things you do well. How could each be used for God?

List the people you see on a typical day. What could you say to each to make his or her day better? What could you do to help them become interested in God?

Obedience

"If being a Christian means I have to obey God, I want no part of it. I don't want to have to obey anyone, especially a God I can't see."

Obedience is not much fun to talk about. However, obeying God is central to growing as a Christian.

Why do Christians think it is worth it to obey God? First, God has the inside information. He knows what he is talking about. He created us and this world. Because he knows the past, the present and the future, he has the information to guide us wisely. He really does know more than we do. It is easier to obey God when we realize that we don't do a very good job running our own lives. We blow it and need help.

Second, God took his own advice. He came to earth and lived as a human, under the same standards he requires of us.

Third, he helps us to do what he asks us to do: he helps us to solve relationships by working on both our attitudes and the attitudes of the other person. He walks with us through the tough temptations and the frustrating, lonely times.

Fourth, obedience to God brings true freedom: for example, always demanding my way keeps me from cooperating with my friends and promotes arguments. "Restricting myself" to consider others' needs as well as my own works out much better.

11
Christian Beliefs: Dispelling the Rumors

○○

There is a great deal of mistaken information floating around about what Christians believe and why they believe it. For example: many people believe that Christians aren't allowed to have any fun. In reality, God is the Creator of laughter and good times. Other people believe that being religious means being silent and bored. Religion can be noisy as well as quiet.

This chapter is intended to clear up some of the incorrect information and the confusion which results.

I'm a Good Person. Do I Still Need Christ?

One of the most commonly believed false rumors about Christianity is that you have to be good to qualify.

Consider the nature of goodness. Goodness is being all God wants us to be. No one lives up to that ideal. We all sin.

Remember from a previous chapter that sin means "missing the mark." Three arrows are aimed toward an archery target. The first arrow comes within an inch of the bull's eye. The second comes within three inches. The third arrow misses the target completely. The first arrow was the closest but it still cannot qualify as a bull's eye.

Similarly, Matthew 19:17 states that only God is good. We can all find somebody worse than us. But when compared with God, we all fall short.

Yes, even though many parts of your life are good, you still need Jesus. Being a Christian is not just a test to pass. It is a relationship with a person who will improve the quality of your life in every way. He will help you with your problems, improve your relationships, give you confidence and purpose, and much more.

Jesus Is the Only Way

"That Christianity stuff is fine if it works for you. It is just not my thing."

Christians feel that religion is not something one shops for like a new dress. One dress can be picked from several, each being equally appropriate. Religion, on the other hand, has more far-reaching consequences. Christians believe that there is only one God and that true religion comes only through a relationship with him. Other religions, including refusal to believe in God, are counterfeits.

If Christianity is real, it affects everyone. God's presence is not something one can choose to ignore. One might decide he didn't want to bother with traffic rules. Soon his car or he would be the victim of a crash. Deciding not to cooperate with other drivers does not change reality. The need for traffic guidelines cannot be wished away. Similarly, the reality of God is something each person must deal with.

Check It Out: Jesus claims to be the only way in John 14:6.

Fun

Christians believe that they know more than anyone else about how to have fun. They are plugged into the source of pleasure—God. They believe that God can best teach people how to have fun.

Christians avoid certain actions which some people consider fun. A few of these are:

- drinking
- vandalism
- sarcasm
- using people
- sex before marriage
- wreckless driving
- drugs

The reason Christians choose not to participate in such activities is that, in the end, they are not really fun. They destroy people, their feelings, and/or their property. They can cause emotional trauma, physical pain, or even death.

These activities genuinely appear fun at first. There is a certain thrill to driving fast or to taking drugs or to having sex without being married. But Christians believe that this is a deception. The pain that can follow is much more powerful than the momentary pleasure.

Many people choose to participate in these destructive types of "fun" activities because "everyone else is doing them." But much of the apparent enjoyment is faked. For example, few people enjoy smoking

Christian Beliefs: Dispelling the Rumors   87

the first time. They talk themselves into enjoying activities that don't really bring pleasure at all.

Christians believe in fun that does not have negative consequences. They believe in pleasure that does not have to be followed by pain. They believe in fun that builds people up, has positive long-term consequences, lasts longer than a moment, and improves health. Some of these are:

- getting to know people
- dating
- kissing
- talking

- eating
- going places
- hugging
- sports

- spending time with friends
- complementing
- sex within marriage

Christians believe that some pleasures are right for some people/ situations and wrong for others. For example:

Eating is fine unless you are on a diet.

Dating is fine unless the person you date is having a negative effect on you.

Talking is fine unless you are interrupting.

Sports are fine unless your attitude is poor.

Dating

"God will understand if I date a non-Christian. After all there aren't any cute Christians at my school."

"Why don't I have a boyfriend? Maybe my standards are too high and I am expecting too much."

"I know he treats me rotten. But I can't get anyone else."

There are two great longings in every person's life. One is the longing for God, and the other is the longing for the opposite sex. Christians believe that only when a person puts God first can the longing for a boyfriend/girl friend be fully satisfied. God loves happy male/female relationships and is very interested in helping Christians find them.

However, if people try to find sweethearts, at the expense of their relationship with God or at the expense of their standards as in the statements above, they sacrifice the quality they might have otherwise had. This can result in misery at worst and frustration at best.

Christian young people spend a great deal of time thinking about dating, planning for it, and worrying about it. In many ways, Christians who date are no different from anyone else. Yet in several ways, they are very different.

First, most Christians feel that they should marry a Christian. One's marriage partner is the most influential person in one's life. If one partner is not a Christian, there will be major conflict: one partner will want to do what God says, and the other will not. The Christian would have to choose between agreeing with the marriage partner and agreeing with God.

Because of the problems of a Christian/non-Christian marriage, many Christians feel that they should date only Christians. One often becomes serious in a relationship before meaning to.

Second, Christians believe that marriage is permanent. Their marriage commitment is a conscious decision to stay with the person no matter what the circumstances. It is the ultimate "for better, for worse," and Christians take it seriously.

Third, Christians believe that they have choices in dating. They believe that they do not "fall" in love like they fall off a mountain. They believe that love is a series of choices and experiences and commitments. In the process of dating, the Christian decides how well she likes the person in different situations. She notices what makes him happy and what brings stress to the relationship. She decides if she would like to face every situation in life with this person. The warm and gooey feelings are a hint that love may be present, but only commitment can keep love there.

Fourth, the main differences between Christian dates and non-Christian dates are the way the guy and girl treat each other and the quality of activities in which they choose to participate.

Christians feel it is important to choose someone who treats them with respect, with whom they can be themselves, and who helps them to become more of the person they are trying to be.

Christians choose activities that encourage them to live the Christian life-style. For example they choose movies with such values as respect for God and other people and healthy enjoyment of life. They choose parties with positive fun. They avoid movies and events which include extramarital sex and violence.

Check It Out: 2 Corinthians 6:14-15 means that Christians should seek other Christians for close relationships, particularly dating and marriage relationships.

First Corinthians 15:33 explains that the type people we choose to date and marry will influence us.

12
Christian Jargon: What It Means

○○○○○○○○○○○○○○○○○○○○○○○○○○○○○○○○○○○○○○

All groups develop their own jargon or words that have special meaning to the group. Here are some words and phrases that have special meaning for Christians.

Accept Jesus or *accept Jesus into your heart*—This phrase means "to become a Christian." The seat of emotions and motivations is often thought of as the "heart." Thus, Christians believe that they must accept Jesus "into their hearts" or into the central guiding part of their lives. The heart is also thought of as the place of love. Christians love Jesus and want Jesus to love others through them.

Amen—This word from both the Old and New Testaments is usually said at the end of prayers, songs, or parts of a worship service. It means "let it be as I have said."

Baptism—Baptism is the act of being immersed in water to symbolize new life in Christ. Jesus himself was baptized and the Bible commands all Christians to be baptized. It is an outward expression of an inward commitment to God. Going under the water symbolizes dying to self-centeredness. Coming out of the water symbolizes entering a new life of Christ-centeredness.

Believe—When Christians say that they "believe in" God or in something he teaches, they mean more than simply that their brain says it is true. Christian belief involves actions and attitudes. One who believes that a chair is strong enough to hold him will sit on that chair. Likewise, someone who believes in God is willing to do whatever he says.

Born again—A popular chapter in the Bible (John 3) describes becoming a Christian as a new birth. Christians are born into a whole new life.

90

Child of God—Christians believe they are born into God's family when they accept a relationship with him. He becomes their parent, and they become his children. It is an intimate and loving relationship with many of the same characteristics of a healthy parent/child relationship.

Christ—"Christ" means "the Anointed One" or the Messiah. These terms mean sent for a special purpose. Jesus Christ was sent by God to "save" or bring the world back to him. "Christ" is often used with "Jesus" as in the previous sentence. It is not Jesus' last name but his title. "Christ" is occasionally used alone to represent Jesus.

Come forward—This phrase means to go to the front of the church to make your commitment to Jesus Christ known to other people. It means the same as "go forward," "go down front," and "walk the aisle." At the end of a church service, a new Christian or a person who wants to become a Christian "comes forward" by leaving his seat and walking down the aisle to the front where the minister stands. There the minister greets him, asks about his decision, and tells the rest of the church about it.

Conversion—This is the transformation from being a non-Christian to being a Christian. Conversion happens when a person decides to invite Jesus to live with her and guide her life.

Conviction—A person "under conviction" is in the process of being convinced that something is right. Non-Christians become "convicted" that Christianity is the only way to live. Christians are "convicted" to begin or stop a certain action.

Disciple—A disciple of Jesus is one who learns from Jesus. Disciples depend on Jesus to teach them how to live. Disciples continue learning throughout their whole lives.

Divine—Divine is an adjective meaning "like God" or referring to God.

Epistle—An epistle is a letter. The Epistles of Paul are the letters he wrote to churches or individuals. Many of the New Testament books are letters.

Everlasting life—This is life that goes on forever. Christians die a physical death, but they then are raised to a new life and live forever with God in a place called heaven.

Faith—Faith is belief, trust, and confidence in God. It expresses itself in action rather than simply with the mind. Christians live out their faith by doing what God asks them to do. Faith includes depending on God for guidance, protection, and salvation.

Forgiveness of sins—"Forgive" means to pardon or to cease to feel resentment toward. God gives new Christians a brand-new start, forgiving all of their past wrongdoing and looking upon them as though they had never sinned. Because all Christians continue to sin, forgiveness continues throughout their lives. God forgives when Christians tell him about their sin and are sorry for it.

Give your heart—This phrase means to commit your life including your emotions, thoughts, actions, and attitudes to Jesus Christ. See "Accept Jesus."

Go forward or *Go down front*—see "Come forward."

God's will—This is what God wants to happen or not to happen. Christians believe that doing what God wants and avoiding what he does not want will bring the greatest happiness and the fewest problems.

Grace—Briefly, grace is "undeserved favor." God cares about us and continues to love us even when we don't deserve it.

Hand of Christian fellowship—This is a welcome to a new Christian from those who are already Christians. Often this is expressed through shaking hands with the new Christian after he has told the church of his decision to become a Christian. See "Come forward."

Heaven—Heaven is the place which God has prepared for Christians after death. It is a place of happiness and enjoyment. There is no sadness or pain there. "Going to heaven" is another way to say, "I'll have eternal life."

Hell—Hell is the place of punishment reserved for persons who do not become Christians. It is a place of eternal separation from God and from other people. Because God is the source of happiness, separation from him means suffering, loneliness, and despair. People decide to spend life after death there by living their lives in a way that ignores God.

Invitation—This is a time at the end of worship services when people are invited to become Christians. Responding to the invitation consists of going to the front of the church and telling the pastor about your decision.

Invite Jesus Christ into your life—See "Accept Jesus."

Justification—Justification's meaning can be easily remembered by dividing the word *justified* like this: "just-*as*-if-ied never sinned." God declares the Christian not guilty and looks upon him as though he had never done any wrong.

Kingdom of God—This is a goal Christians constantly strive for. It is not a place but a state of affairs. The kingdom of God will be present when all people live and treat each other as God would want them to. All will obey God as King.

Kingdom of heaven—See "Kingdom of God."

Lost—Lost is the opposite of "saved" and is one's condition before one becomes a Christian. It means to have no relationship with Jesus Christ. A "lost" person is thus out of touch with all that makes life good.

Personal relationship with Jesus—Christianity is primarily a relationship with the person Jesus Christ. Through this relationship a Christian is reunited with God, is led to live a life that pleases God, and receives the resources (strength, understanding, joy, purpose, etc.) needed to live a complete life.

Prayer—Prayer is talking with God. Christians can pray audibly or silently, alone or in groups.

Profession of faith—To make a profession of faith means to tell others that you have become a Christian and want to live the way Jesus wants you to live. A "profession of faith" is often made at the end of a church service during the "invitation."

Quiet Time—Every day Christians seek to spend some "quiet time" with God. During this time they read the Bible, pray, and think about what God wants them to do that day.

Reconciliation—Through reconciliation, God provides a way for us to "become his friends again." People had made themselves God's enemies by ignoring him, refusing to obey him, and rejecting a relationship with him. Reconciliation happens when God reaches out to a person and that person responds to him.

Redemption—Through redemption, God has purchased us or bought us back. God has purchased us back from the evil that held us and has given us a fresh start. Through him we have the power to begin anew.

Repent—One who repents realizes that living against God is clearly wrong, becomes sorry for this life-style, and decides to completely change over to God's ways. He turns from life without God to life with

God's guidance. Repentance is a beginning step for persons who want to become Christians.

Sanctification—This is God's process through which he guides a Christian to perfection. Christians are on a journey toward being the most complete, happy, and whole people they can be. God is making them into just the people he wants them to be.

Saved—Christians call themselves "saved." They have a relationship with Jesus Christ and are united to God. They are saved from the consequences of life without God. Two of these consequences are unhappy life on earth and eternal separation from God after death in a lonely place of suffering called hell.

Scripture—This is another word for Bible or part of the Bible.

Sin—Doing something wrong ("sin of commission") or failing to do something right ("sin of omission"). Sin is anything against God and his good purposes.

Stewardship—The way one uses one's money, time, and abilities. Christians believe that all that they have belongs to God and that they are responsible to him for how they use each part of it. An example of money/talent stewardship is: giving 10 percent of one's money to the church and leading a Bible study.

Testimony—A Christian's testimony is what Christ has done for that individual. A Christian shares her testimony when she wants you to know about her life in Christ. Usually a testimony includes what her life was like before Christ, how she discovered her need for Christ, how she became a Christian, and what Christ does for her now.

Walk the aisle—See "Come forward."

Washed in the blood—This is a way of saying that one has been forgiven of one's sins by Jesus Christ. Blood is an Old Testament symbol of cleansing. It was believed that an animal must die and its blood must be shed for forgiveness of sins to take place. When Jesus Christ died on the cross, his blood was shed for human forgiveness. A person who accepts Christ's loving forgiveness is said to be washed in the blood of Jesus.

Worship—Worship is any action or attitude that expresses appreciation and love for God. Christians worship through the words they say, through the way they treat others, and through the way they live.

Subject Index

95